Eganridge Inn & Country Club

A lovingly restored English manor Country Inn combining the
perfect blend of century heritage and modern luxury
on a breathtaking setting 5 kms west of Bobcaygeon
on the north shore of Sturgeon Lake.

Acclaimed Casual Dining
Spectacular Golf
Luxurious Accommodations

Eganridge Inn & Country Club

For Reservations with Free Docking
Phone/Fax: (705) 738-5111 • Pro Shop: (705) 738-5115

Eganridge Inn & Country Club
R.R.#3 Fenelon Falls, Ontario K0M 1N0

Four Diamond Award

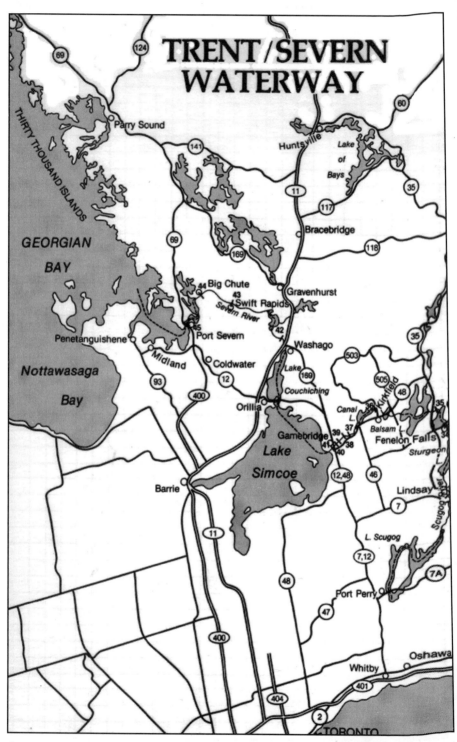

TRENT/SEVERN WATERWAY

THIRTY THOUSAND ISLANDS

GEORGIAN BAY

Nottawasaga Bay

Parry Sound

Penetanguishene

Midland

Coldwater

Big Chute

Swift Rapids

Severn River

Port Severn

Huntsville

Lake of Bays

Bracebridge

Gravenhurst

Washago

Lake Couchiching

Orillia

Gamebridge

Lake Simcoe

Barrie

Canal L.

Kirkfield

Balsam L.

Fenelon Falls

Sturgeon

Lindsay

L. Scugog

Port Perry

Scugog River

Oshawa

Whitby

TORONTO

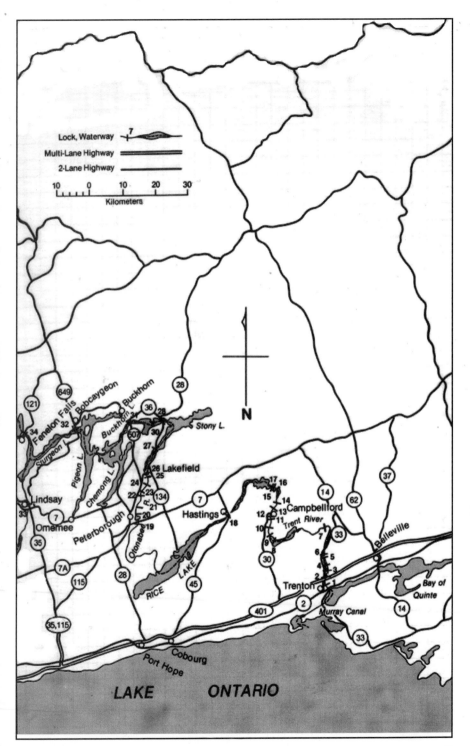

Lock, Waterway
Multi-Lane Highway
2-Lane Highway

10 0 10 20 30
Kilometers

N

649
121
Bobcaygeon
Fenelon Falls
34
32
Buckhorn
Buckhorn L.
36 28
30
27
Stony L.
28
Sturgeon L.
Pigeon L.
Chemong L.
26 Lakefield
25
24
22 23
21
134
Lindsay
33
7
Omemee
Peterborough
20
19
Otonabee
7
Hastings
18
17 16
15 14
12 13 Campbellford
11
10
9
Trent River
7
14
62
37
33
Belleville
6 5
4 3
2
1
35
7A
115
28
RICE LAKE
45
Trenton
30
35,115
401
2
Murray Canal
14
Bay of Quinte
33
Cobourg
Port Hope

LAKE ONTARIO

3

Acknowledgements

● ● ● ● ● ● ● ● ● ● ● ● ● ● ● ● ● ●

We wish to express our thanks to Mr. John Lewis, Superintendent of the Trent-Severn Waterway and his staff for their support of this project.

Our appreciation is also extended to the Friends of the Trent-Severn Waterway. Also, many thanks to the Chambers of Commerce and Tourist Associations along the waterway who have provided us with the most up to date information possible.

Many thanks to those who provided us with the great photos in this edition; Roy Studios, Gord Kilner, Parks Canada-Public Archives, Willy Waterton (GBI), North of Superior, FTSW and other local friends and organizations.

And finally, we would like to thank our advertisers. They have supported the concept of providing a comprehensive directory for boaters on the Trent-Severn Waterway and we hope that, in turn, boaters and other visitors to the Waterway will support them.

Publisher: Lyons Den Enterprizes

Editor: Jenny Ryan

Design & Production: Jenny Ryan

Advertising Sales: Sean Lyons

Copyright ©1998 Ontario Travel Guides
All rights reserved

PO Box 1569
Peterborough, Ontario
K9J 7H7
(705) 745-3974 or 1-800-324-6052

Printed and Bound in Canada

ISBN: 0-9681802-0-5

Welcome to the
Trent-Severn Waterway

Dear Waterway Visitor:

It is my pleasure to welcome you to the Trent-Severn Waterway - one of the most popular vacation destinations in all of Canada. With 44 locks and adjacent park and picnic areas, this national historic canal system and nature corridor provides boaters and car travellers alike with holiday opportunities from Lake Ontario all the way to Georgian Bay and Lake Huron.

As you travel the Waterway, please take the time to visit the lock stations and communities along the way. Here you can experience the rich natural and cultural history of Ontario. The idea of building a 386 kilometre inland navigation route took 87 years to materialize. The dream began in 1833 with a small wooden lock at Bobcaygeon, and with the 1920 completion of Lock #42 near Washago, boat transportation between Lake Ontario and Lake Huron became possible.

Parks Canada, a federal agency within the Department of Canadian Heritage, operates and maintains the Waterway, but many of the services and facilities that will make your trip so enjoyable are provided by private sector businesses and other government agencies located along the canal corridor. This guide is not only an excellent reference source for locating the different services you may require, but is also handy should you wish to plan a holiday around the many events and activities taking place in Waterway communities.

Should you require any information or assistance while visiting a Waterway lock or bridge station, please do not hesitate to speak to the friendly staff. They are well-trained, experienced and committed to making your visit as safe and as pleasant as possible.

John E. Lewis

Superintendent
Trent-Severn Waterway

Canada

Trent/Severn Distance Chart

Approximate
(in miles)

kms x 0.6214 = miles

	TRENTON	FRANKFORD	CAMPBELLFORD	HASTINGS	BEWDLEY	PETERBOROUGH	LAKEFIELD	BURLEIGH FALLS	BUCKHORN	BOBCAYGEON	FENELON FALLS	ROSEDALE	KIRKFIELD	GAMEBRIDGE	ORILLIA	BIG CHUTE
FRANKFORD	8															
CAMPBELLFORD	30	22														
HASTINGS	50	42	20													
BEWDLEY	75	67	45	25												
PETERBOROUGH	90	82	60	40	26											
LAKEFIELD	100	92	70	50	36	10										
BURLEIGH FALLS	113	105	83	73	49	23	13									
BUCKHORN	120	112	90	80	56	30	20	7								
BOBCAYGEON	136	128	106	96	72	46	36	23	16							
FENELON FALLS	150	142	120	110	86	60	50	37	30	14						
ROSEDALE	154	146	124	114	90	64	54	41	34	18	4					
KIRKFIELD	165	157	135	125	101	75	65	52	45	29	15	11				
GAMEBRIDGE	177	169	147	137	113	87	77	64	57	41	27	23	12			
ORILLIA	195	187	165	155	131	105	95	82	75	59	45	41	30	18		
BIG CHUTE	229	221	199	189	165	139	129	116	109	93	79	75	64	52	34	
PT. SEVERN	237	229	207	197	173	147	137	124	117	101	87	83	72	60	42	8

Lake Scugog

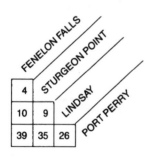

	FENELON FALLS	STURGEON POINT	LINDSAY
STURGEON POINT	4		
LINDSAY	10	9	
PORT PERRY	39	35	26

Lake Simcoe

	ATHERLEY	BARRIE	BEAVERTON	GAMEBRIDGE	LAGOON CITY	JACKSON'S POINT
BARRIE	26					
BEAVERTON	18	26				
GAMEBRIDGE	17	28	3			
LAGOON CITY	11	28	10	7		
JACKSON'S POINT	20	20	13	16	18	
KESWICK	28	22	26	28	28	13

6

Contents

● ● ● ● ● ● ● ● ● ● ● ● ● ● ● ● ● ●

Features

How to Use the Maps

● ● ● ● ● ● ● ● ● ● ● ● ● ● ● ● ● ●

The Waterway maps that are included in this book are designed to correspond with the Trent-Severn Waterway marine charts. The numbers shown on the map pages correspond to the marine chart and sheet numbers.

The maps should be used to locate marinas, public wharfs, locks and towns. The pages describe the facilities and services that are available at the marinas. The mileage information shown on the maps corresponds to the mileage as indicated on the marine charts.

The maps in this book should not be used for navigation purposes.

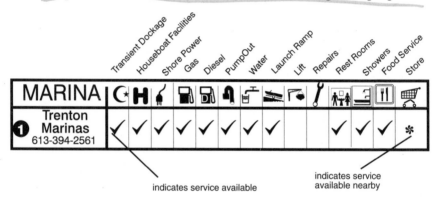

indicates service available

indicates service available nearby

The above chart displays the services provided by each marina. A check below the graphic will indicate that the particular service can be found. The number beside the marina name and address indicates the location on the corresponding map. Navigational draught is 5 feet throughout the system and may be shallower at docks. We recommend contacting the marinas for further information.

Every effort has been made to ensure that the data in this book is accurate. However, changing conditions and incorrect reporting of data make it impossible to guarantee one hundred percent accuracy.

Boaters cruising the Trent-Severn Waterway should purchase appropriate charts to help ensure a safe journey. To travel the system Charts 2021-2029 are required. For assistance in planning a Trent-Severn Waterway vacation call the Friends of the Trent-Severn Waterway's toll-free cruise planning service 1-800-663-2628. Any required charts can be purchased directly from this organization.

Trent-Severn Waterway
At A Glance

●●●●●●●●●●●●●●●●●●

The Trent-Severn Waterway, from Trenton to Port Severn is comprised of four principal river systems in south central Ontario - The Trent, Otonabee, Talbot, Severn - and Rice Lake, the Kawartha Lakes, Lake Simcoe and Lake Couchiching. It visits a number of urban communities such as of Trenton, Peterborough, Lindsay, Barrie and Orillia. It also passes through some archeologically significant areas such as the Petroglyphs and Serpent Mounds, numerous conservation areas and native communities. It also showcases a wealth of human history and an abundance of preserved wildlife.

The Trent-Severn Waterway can be travelled in 7 days if you are interested only in completing a journey. If you are interested in exploring varying terrains, soaking up some of the social histories of each area, taking advantage of waterway hospitality and enjoying some fine fishing, we recommend at least 2 weeks for the return trip. This itinerary is based on 7 days from tip to tip, although your schedule will probably differ depending on your interests and waterway traffic.

You might find it more expedient to arrange your lock-through times during the week to avoid the sometimes heavy weekend traffic that can develop in July and to coincide your stays at waterway towns with festival and fair dates.

The Trent-Severn Waterway is a 240 mile/386 km route which is well marked by sequentially numbered buoys. It is important to note that when you reach the Kirkfield lift lock, the watershed of the Trent-Severn, red and green buoys will be reversed.

This Waterway is within a one day drive of such major urban centres as Montreal, Toronto, Ottawa, Buffalo, Rochester, Cleveland, New York, Syracuse, Albany and Detroit. The Trent-Severn can be accessed by many major highways in Ontario, the 401, Hwy 2, 35, 400, 11, 7a, 7, 12, and 103 as well as U.S. Expressways through Buffalo and the Thousand Islands. By water you can reach the Trent-Severn via the Rideau Waterway, St. Lawrence, Ottawa River, Erie Canal, the Hudson, Lake Champlain, Georgian Bay and the Great Lakes.

DAY ONE

The Trent-Severn is entered at its southern end at Trenton. Visitors arriving from the United States must first contact the customs office by phone, this can be done at Fraser Park Marina on the west side of the river. Trenton boasts a wide array of visitor services, accommodations, restaurants, shopping and excellent marina facilities, at both Centennial Park on the east side of the river and Fraser Park on the west. Both are close to downtown shopping. Fraser Park has gas, diesel and pump-out facilities.

Proceeding upstream through the locks, the urban landscape begins to give way to more rural scenery. The second lock, Sydney, is transected overhead by Highway 401.

From Trenton to Rice Lake, there are 18 locks in all, each having tie-up space and its own special beauty and points of interest. You will not find much in the way of supplies and restaurants until you reach lock 6. From here, it is about a 10 minute walk to the village of Frankford, where you will find restaurants, groceries and a liquor and beer store.

The stretch from lock 7 to locks 11 and 12 at Ranney Falls is fairly secluded and has no groceries or accommodation. From lock 12, it is about 1.25 miles/2 kms to the town of Campbellford. Ferris Provincial Park runs along the east bank of the river. Campbellford has good docking facilities at the town dock, which is about mid-way between locks 12 and 13. Access to all kinds of amenities make Campbellford a good place to stop and explore. Most boaters select to tie up on the concrete wall by the Campbellford Chamber of Commerce and Tourist Information Centre. Here they have convenient access to the shopping district plus shore power and new washroom and shower facilities.

It is 5 miles/8 kms from Campbellford to locks 16 and 17 at Healey Falls. A popular fishing haunt lies here at the powerhouse. The most attractive feature of this site are the falls, just a short walk from the locks. From Healey Falls to Rice Lake it is just less than 20 miles/32 kms. There are plenty of marinas and lodges along the way.

Lock 18 is located at the village of Hastings, where groceries, beer and liquor are available. The tie-up space upstream provides easier access to the town. From Hastings, it is about 6 miles/9.5 kms to Rice Lake.

DAY TWO

Rice Lake is a fairly shallow lake, and is about 16 miles/26 kms long. Rice Lake is famous for fishing. The shallow shorelines and numerous weedbeds make it a popular haunt for muskie and bass. It is also noted as Ontario's top producing lake for walleye. Consult your charts if you are leaving the main channel, especially just north of Harwood. There is a submerged bridge crib from Harwood to the north shore of the lake, which once supported a railroad.

From Rice Lake it is about 20 miles/32 kms upstream to Peterborough and the next lock. Peterborough is the hub of the Trent-Severn Waterway and Parks Canada's Waterway headquarters are located here. Peterborough has a population of approximately 68,000. Thousands of visitors arrive each year to see the workings of lock 21, the hydraulic lift lock opened in 1904. At 65 feet/20 metres, it is the world's highest hydraulic lift lock and is an extremely interesting operation to watch. The Visitor Centre features displays about the construction and operation of the lift lock and general exhibits about the waterway system. Peterborough offers an abundance of accommodation, fine restaurants and shopping.

Locks 22, 23, 24 and 25 are fairly secluded and quiet. You will notice that the countryside is becoming rockier. Lock 26 is downstream of Lakefield but boaters usually tie up at the village's new marina just upstream from the lock on the east bank. Lakefield has a number of good restaurants and excellent shopping facilities and is a key provisioning centre for boaters and cottagers.

DAY THREE

Approximately 1.5miles/2.4 kms upstream, between Katchewanooka Lake and Clear Lake, is the community of Young's Point. The village has a snack bar, restaurants, interesting shopping, post office, marinas and great accommodation.

Continuing up river through Clear Lake, you will note a side trip to the east into Stoney Lake. This is a lovely lake, but there are a lot of rock outcroppings and shoals, so you will want to stay in the channel while sightseeing. Gas and some supplies are available on the south shore of Stoney Lake. Proceeding westward, you will arrive at lock 28 in the hamlet of Burleigh Falls. There used to be two locks at this site, but they were replaced by one large lock. Hence, no lock 29 today. If you are thinking of calling it a day, either Burleigh Falls or Lovesick lock, which is lock 30, might be a good place to tie up for the night. The next lock is Buckhorn, one of the busiest locks on the waterway. You should arrive early to ensure overnight tie-up. From here, you can continue south through Harrington Narrows to arrive at Chemong Lake where the communities of Bridgenorth and Ennismore are located or you can head back to the main channel. The main channel continues westward through Gannon Narrows into Pigeon Lake. This area between Buckhorn and Bobcaygeon is very popular, not only because of its natural beauty but, because there are many side routes to explore and fish without passing through locks. The lock at Bobcaygeon which lifts crafts from Pigeon Lake to Sturgeon Lake was the first lock built on the Trent-Severn Waterway. There is plenty of tie-up space both upstream and downstream of the lock.

DAY FOUR

Another of the original lock sites on the waterway is at Lindsay. This can be reached by following the spur route at the south-western end of Sturgeon Lake and along the Scugog River. The river is narrow and weedy in sections and it is wise to stay in the channel. About 4 miles/6.5 kms into the Scugog River will bring you to lock 33 at Lindsay. The attractive town of Lindsay is surrounded by rolling farmland and boaters can dock right in the heart of downtown at McDonnell Park. Although there are no overnight services here, the beautiful parklands are adjacent to the shopping district and to the Academy Theatre, which presents a number of plays throughout the summer. If you would like to stay overnight, Rivera Park, which you passed just downstream, has overnight facilities and is within walking distance of the downtown core. It is about a 15 minute walk. (A side trip to the town of Port Perry via Lake Scugog will take you past Scugog Island, home of the new Great Blue Heron Charitable Casino.)

Retracing your steps to Sturgeon Lake, continue north to lock 34 at Fenelon Falls. Because this is such a busy spot, you may have trouble docking. The blue line area at the lock is strictly for through-locking traffic. There is docking upstream of the lock at the railway bridge. Scenic Fenelon Falls is a great spot for shopping and services and for walking and browsing.

DAY FIVE

The village of Rosedale is 4 miles/6.5 kms upstream which is also very busy, and has a lot of accommodation and a number of marinas. From Rosedale, you can continue through lock 35 into Balsam Lake. If you are interested in exploring the village of Coboconk and its many shops and services, you can proceed north from Rosedale through Balsam Lake to the Gull River. Otherwise you can follow the main channel from Rosedale across Balsam Lake, south of Grand Island. The stretch from Balsam Lake to Lake Simcoe is comprised of 6 different locks, the highest of which is the lift lock at Kirkfield. Kirkfield's hydraulic lift lock is the second highest in North America. This site is the watershed of the Trent-Severn, boaters will have to remember that red and green buoys are reversed and you are now travelling downstream. There are 5 locks in quick succession along the Talbot River before entering Lake Simcoe. The run from Gamebridge to the narrows between Lakes Simcoe and Couchiching is about 15 miles/24 kms. Simcoe is the largest lake on the waterway and boasts terrific deep-water cruising. Ports of call include Beaverton, Pefferlaw, Jackson's Point, Keswick, Lagoon City and Barrie. Check weather conditions and with the lockmaster before crossing Lake Simcoe, this is big water.

Orillia, on the south-west coast of Couchiching, is one of the boating hot-spots on the waterway. Since the waterfront was renovated, there are now over 200 slips for transient boaters. Across from the docks is Mississaga Street, the main street in Orillia. Restaurants, a liquor store, banks, hardware store and accommodation are within a short walk from the docks. Don't forget to visit Casino Rama!

DAY SIX

The narrows at the head of Lake Simcoe open into Lake Couchiching. This lake is approximately 10 miles/16 kms long and 3 miles/4.8 kms wide. As on Lake Simcoe, storms can blow up very suddenly, it is wise to listen to the marine forecast before leaving port. Heading north you will pass Chief Island, which has a large sandy cove on the north shore. From Chief Island, it is about 7 miles/11 kms to the north tip of Lake Couchiching and another mile or so to lock 42. Lock 42 has lovely surroundings and is a quiet spot for overnight docking. The channel along here is quite narrow for 4 miles/6.5 kms until it opens into Sparrow Lake. This lake is primarily cottage country although there is a general store, snack bar and gas pump at the federal dock in the resort community of Port Stanton. The northern part of Sparrow Lake is quite reedy and the surrounding land flat, but once into the Severn River, the terrain changes dramatically to granite cliffs. From here to Port Severn, the scenery is unrivaled. Lock 43 at Swift Rapids is the largest on the waterway. This is a secluded locksite.

7 DAY SEVEN

Approximately 2.5 miles/4 kms downstream of lock 43 is the hamlet of Severn Falls, where there is a marina, grocery store, general store, and restaurant. From here it is only 5 miles/8 kms to Big Chute Marine Railway which is one of the major thrills of the waterway. The channel downstream of Big Chute is very narrow and winding. Boaters travelling upstream should give downstream boaters the right of way, because they are being propelled by the current and it is difficult to manoeuvre.

Once you have passed this short channel, you will be in Gloucester Pool. The pool has numerous coves and inlets to explore. Consult your charts, as some areas have rock outcroppings and shoals. A popular fishing spot is at the foot of the dam at the western end of White's Bay. It is a short run from Gloucester Pool to Port Severn where Georgian Bay begins. Lock 45 at Port Severn has been renovated and expanded and offers excellent facilities for overnight docking. There is good tie-up space on the upstream side of the lock and a number of good marinas offering full service before heading out on Georgian Bay.

Although this is the completion of the Trent-Severn Waterway, this last lock-through is also the beginning of Georgian Bay....another superb area to cruise and explore.

In this edition of the *Trent-Severn Boating and Road Guide* we have taken the opportunity of introducing our readers to the North Channel and North of Superior regions which offer boaters and other visitors tremendous waterway vacations. Please see Area 9 for details.

Getting There

●●●●●●●●●●●●●●●●●●●

The southern gateway to the Trent-Severn Waterway at Trenton is a popular access point to this historic canal system for boaters cruising from the United States or other regions of Ontario and Quebec. The major east-west Highway 401 on Trenton's northern outskirts provides convenient access to visitors trailering their boats or exploring by car or camper. It's said that half the fun of a vacation is getting there and an adventure cruise on the Trent-Severn Waterway is no exception. Boaters approaching Trenton from the east along the Bay of Quinte or the west on Lake Ontario and the connecting Murray Canal will be treated to several key welcoming communities offering all required provisions and excellent overnight marina services.

Belleville: Billed as "the choice location", Belleville offers big city amenities along with small town friendliness, and a pleasing mixture of the historic and modern. Located on the Bay of Quinte this is home to an excellent yacht harbour which is a picturesque stopping point for Great Lakes sailors, and a favourite launch for sportfishing enthusiasts after walleye, pike and bass. In the winter Belleville becomes a major ice fishing centre. Each July thousands of visitors enjoy the Waterfront Festival & Folklorama, while year round beautiful music chimes from City Hall clock tower overlooking the new civic square and farmers market.

Belleville is an award winning 'Community in Bloom', with floral displays throughout the City's park system, thousands of roses in Corby Park, and an autumn extravaganza of Chrysanthemums in

Meyer's Pier During Waterfront Festival and Folklorama

15

Riverside Park. Visitors will also find the city convenient to the Bay of Quinte region with its beaches, museums, bird migrations, racing facilities, factory outlets and First Nations attractions. Touring is a fascinating adventure along the Loyalist Parkway, the Cheese Route and the Apple Route all nearby. Belleville is conveniently located on Hwy 401, and is definitely worth a visit. Belleville offers excellent hotels, motels, campgrounds, marinas, picnic areas and fine restaurants. Docking facilities are located adjacent to the downtown core giving boaters access to every shopping need.

Cobourg: When approaching the Murray Canal and Trenton from the west, boaters can dock at several welcoming ports that will offer excellent overnight docking accommodations for provisions and fuel or safety during rough weather. Cobourg is situated on a sandy stretch of Lake Ontario shoreline. A vibrant and charming community, this town has a rich and intriguing history enthusiastically expressed in the splendid heritage buildings around town. Boaters can enjoy a leisurely walk to fine stores and restaurants in the downtown area, just 5 minutes from the marina or for added convenience bicycles are available free of charge at the marina office. Cobourg displays friendly small town charm, offering visitors a multitude of things to do and see, including summer concerts in Victoria Park and exceptional shows in magnificent Victoria Hall.

The Hall boasts 41 rooms including the elegant concert hall, the old Bailey Court House and the Art Gallery of Northumberland. Guided

Cobourg Harbour

tours are offered during the summer or special tours can be arranged through the Chamber of Commerce. The visitor information centre is located in Dressler House, 212 King Street West (905-372-5831) birthplace of 1930's Oscar winning actress Marie Dressler. The friendly staff would be happy to provide a conducted tour of the house.

Beautiful Victoria Park, adjacent to Heritage Harbour offers an amazing array of activities for visitors of all ages, lawn bowling, band concerts, mini golf, children's playground, wading pool, outdoor swimming pool and a great clean sandy beach. Victoria Park is the venue for the Cobourg Waterfront Festival of Arts, Crafts and Entertainment held annually over the Canada Day Weekend. The newly constructed boardwalk creates an extremely pleasant walk linking Heritage Harbour, the campground and Victoria Park. Cobourg is a hub of activities during the summer season. Call the Chamber of Commerce at (905-372-5831) or (1-888-COBOURG) for details and a calendar of events.

Boat Haulers in Action

Brighton & Presqu'ile Park

●●●●●●●●●●●●●●●●●●

Brighton is known as the Gateway to Presqu'ile. Just west of Trenton on Presqu'ile Bay, it's your last port on Lake Ontario before entering the Murray Canal. While in Brighton make sure you visit Proctor House. Equipped with its own ghost, this historical home stands sentinel on the hill overlooking Presqu'ile Bay.

Presqu'ile Park is renowned for its birding. Birding events include conducted walks, telescope stations staffed by naturalists and summer youth naturalist programs. You can camp here at what has been called the quintessential summer playground, with all amenities including a store, museum and special programs. Call (613) 475-2204 for details.

To the east, the Murray Canal with its two swing bridges is the entrance from Lake Ontario to the Trent-Severn Waterway and the Bay of Quinte.

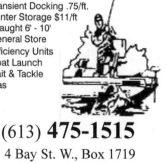

Dockside Dining Guide

RD	Resort Dining
Fam	Family Dining
FF	Fast Food
Lic	Licensed by the L.L.B.O.

Morch Marine Patio & Restaurant Fam, Lic *Belleville*

Trenton Marina - Patio & Snack Bar FF *Trenton*

Hearthside Dining Room RD,Lic 1-800-461-1940 Elmhirst Resort, *Keene -Rice Lake*

Wild Blue Yonder Pub & Coffee Shop Fam, Lic 1-800-461-1940 Elmhirst Resort, *Keene Rice Lake*

Victoria Inn RD, Lic (905)-342-3261 Next to Cox'ies Cove, *Gore's Landing- Rice Lake*

Riverside Grill & Gazebo - Holiday Inn Fam, Lic (705)743-1144 *Peterborough Waterfront*

The Electric Clove Fam, Lic (705)876-6721 25 George St. *Peterborough* (across from Marina)

Olde Stone Brewing Co. Fam, Lic (705)745-0495 380 George St. N, *Peterborough*

The Galley FF Peterborough Marina -*Little Lake*

Old Bridge Inn Hotel RD, Lic 705-652-8507 *Young's Point - Lock 27*

Whetung's Tea Room Fam Whetung Ojibwa Art Gallery *Curve Lake*

The Big Tomato RD, Lic Bobcaygeon Inn Front & Main Streets 705-738-5433 *Bobcaygeon - Lock 32*

Harbour Doc's Seafood Restaurant Fam, Lic Gordon Yacht Harbour 705-738-2381 81 Front St., *Bobcaygeon Lock 32*

Mac's Long Beach Marina - Fam, Breakfast, Lunch *Sturgeon Lake*

Eganridge Inn & Country Club RD, Lic 705-738-5111
North Shore Sturgeon Lake, btwn Bobcaygeon & Fenelon Falls

Dockside Grill Fam, Lic
12 Water St. *Fenelon Falls - Lock 34*

The Country Cupboard
Ice Cream, Specialty Items
9 May Street *Fenelon Falls - Lock 34*

Dirty Harry's Roadhouse
Taggarts Landing Restaurant RD, Lic 705-887-9000   *Fenelon Falls - Lock 34*

Sundial Restaurant Fam, Lic. 157 Lindsay St.
Fenelon Falls

The Chatterbox Patio & BBQ Fam, Lic 705-887-1414
21 Francis St. W. *Fenelon Falls - Lock 34*

The Pattie House Fam, Lic
705-454-2100 *Coboconk - Balsam Lake*

The Galley Harbourside
Fam. *Beaverton Harbour*

Neptune's Bistro Fam, Lic
705-484-0800 *Lagoon City Marine Centre - Lake Simcoe*

Big Bay Point Yacht Club
Fam, Lic 1-800-565-2745
Lake Simcoe

City of Barrie Marina Restaurant *Barrie - Lake Simcoe*

Orillia Square Mall
New York Fries FF
Burger King FF
Mrs. Vanelli's FF
Hwy#11 at Burnside Line, Orillia

Gramma's Lunch Restaurant
Ojibway Bay Marina Fam
Lake Couchiching

Silver Pines Restaurant & Patio Fam, Lic (705)-689-2813
Kilworthy - Sparrow Lake

Big Chute Marina Restaurant   Fam, Lic "top of the chute" - *Lock 44*

Rawley Lodge - RD, Lic
1-800-263-7538 *Port Severn, Lock 45*

Inn at Christie's Mill - RD, Lic. 1-800-465-9966   *Port Severn, Lock 45*

Severn Boat Haven Snack Bar FF, Port Severn - Lock 45

Midland Harbour Restaurant   Fam, Lic *Midland Harbor*

Captain Roberts' Table
Fam,Lic. (705)549-8064 *Discovery Harbour Penetaguishene*

Accommodation Guide

●●●●●●●●●●●●●●●●●●●

The Trent-Severn Waterway is host to a range of accommodation from modest Bed and Breakfast to four diamond resort, from motels and self-catering cottages to romantic Victorian Inns.

Harbour View Motel & Marina 4 Bay St. W. BOX 1719, Brighton, On K0K 1H0 (613) 475-1515

Campbellford River Inn - Trent River Box 569, Campbellford, On K0L 1L0 (705) 653-1771 or 1-800-984-6665 *20 rooms overlooking the Trent River* - docking

Sandercock's Tourist Resort Rice Lake R.R. #2 Roseneath Box 71, On K0K 2X0 (905)352-2469 *Cottages, trailer space*

Victoria Inn- South Side of Rice Lake Harwood Road & Burnham St,. Gore's Landing, On K0K 2E0 (905)342-3261 email: VictoriaInn@eagle.caWebsite:www.eagle.ca/VictoriaInn *Lakeside Country Inn* -(docking (next door at Cox'ies Cove)

Elmhirst Resort -North Side of Rice Lake R.R. #1 Keene, On K0L 2G0 (705)295-4591 1-800-461-1940 email: elmhirst@cycor.ca *Luxury Resort - Self-Catering Cottages* - docking

Best Western Otonabee - Otonabee River 84 Lansdowne

St. E., Box 366, Peterborough, On, K9G 6Z5 (705)742-3454 *Resort Like Setting in the City* - docking (draft 3.5')

Holiday Inn - Waterfront Little Lake -beside Peterborough Marina 150 George St. N., Peterborough, On, K9J 3G5 (705)743-1144 , 1-800-465-4329 *Hotel Accommodation* - docking

Old Bridge Inn Hotel - Lock 32 Young's Point, On K0L 3G0 (705)652-8507 *Old Fashioned Country Hotel Bed & Breakfast*

Viamede Resort Mt. Julian, Stoney Lake (705) 652-1166 *Resort & Conference Centre*

Irwin Inn Crowes Landing, Stoney Lake R.R.#2 Lakefield, On, K0L 2H0 (705) 877-2240, 1-800-461-6490 *Country Inn & cottages*

Sunrise Resort - Just below lock 31 P.O. Box 85, Buckhorn, On K0L 1J0 (705)657-8713 *Cottages and Motel*

Eganridge Inn & Country Club - Sturgeon Lake R.R. #3 Fenelon Falls, K1M 1N0 (705)738-5111 *English Manor Country Inn* - docking

The Rhubarb Patch B & B - Minutes from Lock 34 -30 Oak St., Fenelon Falls, On (705)887-9586 *Victorian Bed and Breakfast*

The Olde Rectory B & B - Minutes from Lock 34 54 Louisa, Fenelon Falls, On (705)887-9796 *Victorian Bed and Breakfast*

Sundial Motel - Minutes from Lock 34 157 Lindsay St., Fenelon Falls, On (705)887-2400 *family, motel accommodation*

Fenelon Inn - Short distance from Lock 34 Fenelon Falls, On (705)887-9000 *Luxury Accommodation*

Port of Call Marina & Motel Bolsover - before Lock 37 R.R. #6, Box 407 Woodville, On K0M 2T0 (705)426-7522 *motel* - docking

Sir William McKenzie Inn P.O. Box 255, Kirkfield, On K0M 2B0 (705)438-1278 Historic *Country Inn*

Betty & Tony's Waterfront B & B - Atherley Narrows 677 Broadview Ave., Orillia, On L3V 6P1 (705)326-1125 or 1-800-308-2579 Website: www.bbcanada.com/9.html email:tonybridgens@encode.com *Bed & Breakfast* - docking

Pan O Rama - *Bed & Breakfast* on Lake Couchiching 622 Moberley Ave, Orillia, On L3V 6R6 (705)326-1636-docking

Forest Glen Resort - Hamlet Swing Bridge, near Sparrow LakeR.R. #1 Severn Bridge, On P0E 1N0 (705)689-2904 Cottages - docking

Inn at Christie's Mill - Lock 45 Box 125, Port Severn, On L0K 1S0 (705)538-2354 or 1-800-465-9966 *Lakeside Country Inn* -docking

Driftwood Cove Marine Resort - Lock 45 P.O. Box 264, Port Severn, On K0K 1S0 (705)538-2505 *Housekeeping Units and Cottages* - docking

Rawley Lodge - Lock 45 Box 189, Port Severn, On L0K 1S0 1-800-263-7538 *Country Inn & Resort* - docking

Bayview-Wildwood Resort- Port Stanton-R.R. #1 Severn Bridge, On P0E 1N0 1-888-422-9843 *Country Resort*-near wharf

Shopping & Services Guide

Cobourg IGA
270 Spring St. Cobourg   Minutes from Cobourg Harbour *Grocery Store*

Hastings Marine & The Boat House-Front St. Hastings *Boat Sales, Rentals & Marine Supplies*

Boater's World
216 Rink St. Peterborough (705)745-3029 *Marine Supplies*

Century 21/Gray Munro Realty   Peterborough (705)743-6666 *Dave Carter*

Plum Loco 373 George St. N Peterborough *Neat Clothing & Accessories*

Cottage Toys Charlotte St. , Peterborough *Sales & Rentals (705)741-2150* (Outlets in Lakefield, Bridgenorth)

Lockside Trading Co. - Lock 27 Young's Point *Furniture, Country Items, Gifts, Cottage Outfitters - Largest Country Store in the Kawarthas*

Whetung Ojibway Crafts & Art Gallery - Coppaway Point Curve Lake Indian Reserve- *Art Gallery and Crafts*

Kawartha Park Marine - Stoney Lake *Marine & Grocery Supplies*

Reach Harbour - Lower

Buckhorn   *Grocery Supplies*

Twenty May Street - Lock 34 Fenelon Falls *Quality Clothing & Accessories*

Chelsea Bun Bakery - Lock 34 25 Colborne St. Fenelon Falls *Baked Goods*

Fenelon Falls IGA - Lock 34 Across from Locks, Fenelon Falls *Grocery Store*

Sunshine Freshmart
48 Colborne St. Fenelon Falls *Grocery Store*

Purse Strings - Lock 34 42 Colborne St, Fenelon Falls *Consignment Clothing*

Village Barber Shop - Lock 34   42 Colborne St., *Fenelon Falls*

Sneakers Etc. - Lock 34 3 Francis St. W Fenelon Falls *Family Footwear*

Shutterbug Photofinishing - Lock 34   3 Francis St. W., Fenelon Falls *Cameras & Accessories*

Trail and Street - Lock 34 16 May Street Fenelon Falls *Footwear*

Canadian Tire -Lock 34 Fenelon Falls *Marine Supplies, Sporting Goods, Hardware*

Bookfinder - Lock 34
32 Colborne Fenelon Falls
Books, New & Used

**Forster's Antiques And
Collectibles** - Hwy 121 Fenelon
Falls

Stokes on Trent
8-10 Colborne Fenelon Falls
Jewellery, China Gifts

Kathy's Pet Foods
4B May St. Fenelon Falls

Fenelon Pet Supplies
51 Colborne Fenelon Falls

Stinson Pharmacy
53 Colborne St. Fenelon Falls

**Fenelon Cleaners &
Laundromat** - 16 Market St.
Fenelon Falls

Bowes & Cocks Ltd. Realty
29 Colborne St. Fenelon Falls
1-800-241-0667

Coboconk IGA - Balsam Lake
Coboconk *Grocery Store*

Bowes & Cocks Ltd. Realty
Main Street Coboconk
1-800-241-0667

**Tri-County Building
Supplies/True Value Hardware**
Hwy 35 Coboconk *Hardware
Store*

**Canadian Imperial Bank of
Commerce** Coboconk *instant
teller*

Big Bay Point Marina - West
Shore Lake Simcoe *Marine &
Grocery Supplies*

Forest Glen Resort -Hamlet
Swing Bridge near Sparrow Lake
General Store

Big Chute Marina - Lock 44
Marine *Supplies & General Store*

Driftwood Cove-Lock 45 Port
Severn *Marine Supplies*

Plum Loco 114 Mississaga St.
E. Orillia *Clothing & Accessories*

The Bird House Nature Co.
165 Mississaga St. E, Orillia
Birding supplies, expert advice

Orillia Square Mall
*Shoppers Drug Mart
Zehr's Markets
Japan Camera
K-Mart*
Hwy #11 at Burnside Line

Severn Boat Haven - Lock 45
Port Severn *Grocery Store &
Marine Supplies*

More machines for your money while cruising the Trent-Severn Waterway.

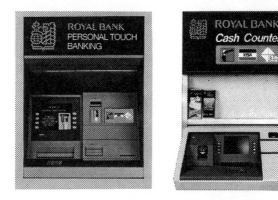

Visit one of our Automated Banking Machines for fast cash, while you cruise the Trent-Severn Waterway:

- Trenton
- Campbellford
- Port Perry
- Peterborough
- Lakefield

- Buckhorn
- Bobcaygeon
- Lindsay
- Orillia
- Washago

Canada's leader in self-serve banking

 ROYAL BANK

Please Don't Drink and Boat

Enjoy Your Summer

The Beer Store

The Beer Store

Location	Hours of Sale-Summer	Distance from System
Trenton 49 Byron St. (613)392-5663	10:00am - 8:00pm daily Thurs/Fri 10:00am-10:00pm Sat 9:00am - 10:00pm	within 1 mile
Hastings Front St (705)696-2871	10:00am -6:00pm daily Fridays 10:00am-9:00pm Sat 10:00am-9:00pm	within 1 mile
Peterborough 139 George St. N. (705)742-8171	10:00am - 9:00pm daily Friday 9:30am - 9:00pm	within 1 mile
Lakefield Queen St. (705)652-3031	10:00am - 6:00pm daily Friday 10:00am - 9:00pm	within 1 mile
Bridgenorth Ward St. (705)292-7126	10:00am - 6:00pm daily Friday 10:00am - 9:00pm	within 1 mile
Bobcaygeon 25 King St. E. (705)738-3596	10:00am - 7:00pm daily Fri 10:00am -10:00pm Sat 9:30am-10:00pm	within 1 mile
Fenelon Falls 125 Lindsay St. (705)887-3222	10:00am - 9:00pm daily Fri 10:00am - 10:00pm Sat 9:30am - 6:00pm	within 1 mile
Lindsay 370 Kent St. E. (705)324-3541	10:00am - 6:00pm daily Fri 10:00am - 9:00pm Sat 9:30am-10:00pm	Approx. 2 miles
Port Perry 677 Queen St. (905)985-2322	10:00am - 6:00pm daily Fri 10:00am - 9:00pm Sat 9:30am - 6:00 pm	within 1 mile
Campbellford 80 Centre St. (705)653-1220	10:00am - 6:00pm daily Fri 10:00am - 9:00pm 9:30am - 9:00pm	Slightly over 1 mile
Coboconk Highway #35 (705)454-8983	10:00am - 6:00pm daily Fri 10:00am - 9:00pm	within 1 mile
Beaverton 553 Mara Rd. (705)426-7341	10:00am - 6:00pm daily Fri 10:00am - 9:00pm	approx. 1/2 mile

The Beer Store (cont'd)

Location	Hours of Sale-Summer	Distance from System
Keswick 299 the Queensway (905)476-4581	10:00am - 10:00pm daily	approx. 1/2 mile
Sutton Dalton Rd. (905)722-3341	10:00am - 10:00pm	within 1/2 mile
Barrie 299 Blake St. (705)726-1662	10:00am - 6:00pm daily Thur/Fri 10:00am - 9:00pm Sat 9:30am - 6:00pm	approx. 1/2mile
Orillia 275 Atherley Rd. (705)326-6483	10:00am - 9:00pm daily Thur/Fri 10:00am - 10:00pm Sat 9:30am - 11:00pm	approx 2 miles
Penetang 19 PenetanguisheneRd. (705)549-2519	10:00am - 6:00pm daily Fri 10:00am - 9:00pm	approx 2 miles
Midland 293 Midland Ave. (705) 526-5211	10:00am - 6:00pm daily Fri 10:00am - 9:00pm Sat 9:30 am - 9:00pm	approx 2 miles

Store hours are subject to change.

Liquor Control Board of Ontario Outlets

Town Location	Address	Telephone
Trenton	34 Ford St.	(613) 392-3797
Frankford Comb.(Liq&Beer)	6 King St.	(613) 398-6160
Campbellford	37 Front St.	(705)653-3000
Hastings	18 Front St. W	(705)696-2291
Bewdley	5087 Rice Lake Dr.N.	(905)797-2077
Peterborough	196 Sherbrooke	(705) 745-1333
Lakefield	Nichols &Water Sts.	(705)652-7031
Buckhorn	Combination Liquor/Beer Store	(705)657-3211
Bridgenorth	Ward St.	(705)292-9801
Omemee Comb.(Liq/Beer) Store	King St.	(705)799-5212
Bobcaygeon	37 King St. E.	(705) 738-2591
Lindsay	35 Russel St. W	(705)324-5511
Port Perry	135 Perry St.	(905)985-2392
Fenelon Falls	27 Francis St. W.	(705)887-3220
Coboconk	7 Albert St.	(705)454-3992
Beaverton	336 Bay St.	(705)426-7373
Sutton	High St. Plaza	(905)722-3641
Keswick	184 Simcoe St.	(905)476-5322
Barrie	279 Yonge St. #16	(705)739-0162
Orillia	201 MississagaSt. E.	(705)326-6591
Port Severn	3238 Old Port Severn Rd.	(705)538-2854
Victoria Harbour	144 Albert St.	(705)534-3626
Honey Harbour	Honey Harbour Rd.	(705)756-2593
Penetang	Village Square	(705)549-2526
Midland	436 Bay St. E.	(705)526-6911

All stores are within a short walk (5-10 minutes) from waterway. Lindsay outlet is a 20 minute walk. Hours vary from store to store, all stores open at 9:30 am.

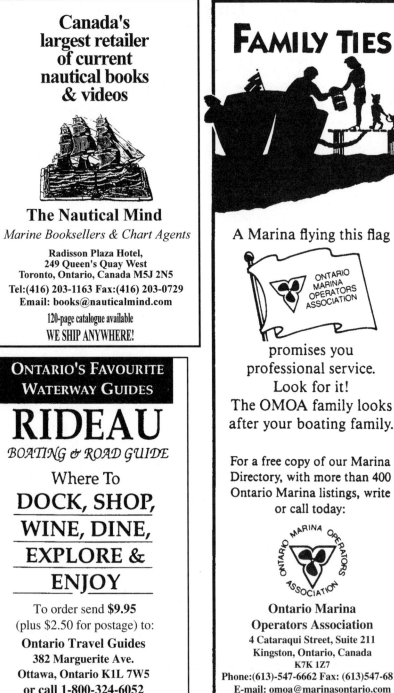

Fairs and Festivals

May

Orillia Perch Festival **Port of Orillia** Mid April - Mid May

Kiwanis Walleye World Fishing Derby **Trenton** Early May

Navigation Season Opens **Trent-Severn Waterway** Long Wknd

Main Street Spring Fling **Bobcaygeon** Mid May

Pioneer Sheep and Wool Craft **Lang Pioneer Village** 3rd weekend

Home and Recreation Show **Fenelon Falls Arena** Early May

Canada/U.S.Walleye Tournament **Bobcaygeon** Late May

Annual Soap Box Derby & Fireworks **Frankford** long weekend

Victoria Day Fireworks **Peterborough** long weekend

Kawartha Walleye Challenge **Rice Lake** long weekend

Victoria Days **Lakefield** long weekend

Greatest Garage Sale Under the Sun **Orillia** long weekend

"Two Weeks in May...& then some" Arts Festival **Belleville** Mid May

Spring Craft Show **Buckhorn** Mid May

Annual Muskoka Fun Run Series **Port of Orillia** Mid May

Annual Canoe Festival **Peterborough** Mid May

Christmas Shop Opens **Whetung Ojibwa Crafts & Art Gallery**

Open House **Whetung Ojibwa Crafts & Art Gallery** Mid May

Home & Recreation Show **Fenelon Falls** Mid May

June

Canoe the Nonquon/Boat Blessing Service **Port Perry** Early June

Spring Flea Market **Barrie** Early June

Victorian Flower Show **Lang Pioneer Village** Mid June

Heritage Festival **Lang Pioneer Village** Late June

Settlers' Days **Kawartha Settlers' Village, Bobcaygeon** Late June

Rose Show **Cobourg** Late June

Pioneer Picnic **Pefferlaw** 2nd Saturday

Georgina Highland Games **Keswick** 3rd weekend

Marsh Mash Marathon Canoe & Kayak Race **Bradford** Mid June

Quinte International Air Show 1998) **Trenton** last weekend

Bass Tournament **Port Perry** last weekend

Hurdville Parry Sound Canoe Race **Parry Sound** last weekend

Mariposa Folk Festival **Barrie** last weekend

Bass Tournament **Midland** last weekend

Masters Annual Walleye Fishing **Buckhorn**(Sunrise Resort)

Children's Fishing Derby **Buckhorn** (Sunrise Resort)

Lobsterfest **Fenelon Falls** Late June

Waterfront Festival **Cobourg** Late June

Annual Ducks Unlimited Golf Tournament **Eganridge Golf & Country Club** Early June

Museum Strawberry Social **Fenelon Falls** Late June

Vintage Classic Country Car Show **Lakefield** Mid June

Annual Traditional Pow Wow **Lovesick Lake** Mid June

Blooming Art Exhibition **Orillia** Sir Sam Steele Art Gallery

Marine Day **Buckhorn Locks** Mid June

Annual Arts & Crafts Show **Fenelon Falls** Late June

'Christmas In June' **Port of Orillia** Mid June

Giant In Water Used Boat Show **Port Of Orillia** Mid June

Marine Safety Awareness Show **Port of Orillia** Mid June

East Lake Simcoe Pioneer Society Steam Show **Fenelon Falls** Mid June - Mid July

Georgian Bay Heritage Festival **Penetanguishene** Mid June

Antique and Collectibles Show & Sale **Beaverton** Mid June

Beaverton Bass Derby **Beaverton Harbour** Late June

Festival of Lights **Peterborough** Mid June to Mid August(Wed. & Sat. evenings)

Festival of Lights, Crary Park Peterborough

July

Canada Day Celebrations

Canada Day **Buckhorn**

Canada Day **Lakefield**

Canada Day **Orillia**

Canada Day **Trenton**

Multicultural Festival **Peterborough** Canada Day Weekend

Tunnel Boat Races and Fishing Derby **Campbellford** 1st weekend

Settlers' Days **Sutton** Canada Day Weekend

Art in the Park **Jackson's PointLake Simcoe**) Canada Day Wknd

Waterfront Fireworks **Port Perry** Canada Day July 1

Festivities **Lindsay** Canada Day July 1

Rotary Club B.B.Q. **Midland** Canada Day July 1

Waterfront Festival **Cobourg** Canada Day July 1

Celebration and Fireworks **Fenelon Falls** Canada Day July 1

Pioneer Days Celebration **Omemee** Canada Day Weekend

Fireworks & Activities **Penetanguishene** Canada Day Weekend

Arts & Crafts Show **Bobcaygeon** Canada Day Weekend

Ducks Unlimited Banquet & Auction **Bobcaygeon** Canada Day

Celebrations **Beaverton** Canada Day

July

Summer Arts Festival **Beaverton**   early July - Labour Day

Rice Lake B.B.Q. **Bewdley**   1st weekend

Highland Games   **Cobourg**   1st weekend

Triathlon   **Jackson's Point**   2nd Sunday

Open Fiddle And Step Dance Competition   **Midland**   2nd weekend

Hot Air Balloon Championships   **Barrie**   1st or 2nd week

Festival Days   **Port Perry**   2nd weekend

Antique and Nostalgia Show   **Campbellford**   2nd weekend

Lions Club Sunshine Festival   **Fenelon Falls**   2nd Sunday

Rice Lake Bass Tournament   **Bewdley**   2nd weekend

Quilt Show and Sale   **Campbellford**   2nd weekend

Art in the Park   **Parry Sound**   2nd or 3rd weekend

Canoe Tour -Osprey Walk **Ken Reid Conservation Area Lindsay**
Mid July

Take a Hike/Take a Cruise-Parks Day **Waterway Wide: Ferris,
Peterborough, Petroglyphs, Lindsay, Balsam, Big Chute**
3rd Weekend (Contact FTSW for info.)

Harvey Township Heritage Day   **Lang Pioneer Village** Mid July

"Blooms of Summer" Garden Tour **Lindsay** 2nd weekend

Arts and Craft Show and Sale   **Coboconk**   2nd week

Annual Fiddle & Step Dance Contest   **Bobcaygeon** Late July

Liberty Days   **Penetanguishene**   3rd or 4th weekend

Molson Highland Games   **Barrie**   4th weekend

Festival of the Sound   **Parry Sound**   Late July - Mid August

Antique Show & Sale **Lindsay** Mid July

River Festival   **Lindsay**   Last Weekend

Waterfront Festival & Folklorama   **Belleville**   Mid July

Ontario Family Fishing Weekend   **Campbellford**   Early July

Indian Cycle Day   **Campbellford**   Early/Mid July

Annual Antique & Nostalgia Show   **Campbellford**   Mid July

Festival Weekend   **Coboconk**   Late July

Highland Games   **Cobourg**   Early July

Lakeside Antique & Classic Cars)   **Cobourg** Early July

Canadian Country Jamboree   **Hastings**   Mid July

Top Bass Fishing Tournament   **Hastings**   Mid July

Reel Fish'n Competition   **Hastings**   Late July

Annual Rice Lake Bass Tournament   **Keene**   Mid July

"Remembering Margaret" Festival **Lakefield**   Mid July

Lakefield Fair   **Lakefield**   Late July

Centre of Power Poker Run **Port of Orillia**   Mid July

Annual Summer Festival   **Trenton**   Mid July

Promenade Days Street Festival   **Barrie-Downtown**   Early July

Orillia Scottish Festival   **Orillia**   Mid July

Annual Arts & Crafts Show **Orillia Square Mall** Mid July

English Teas **Orillia Leacock Museum** July   August

Leacock Heritage Festival **Orillia** Mid July- Mid Aug

CANATS '97 **Trenton** July 4-6, 1997

Exhibition **Peterborough** Early July

August

Gathering of the Clans **Parry Sound** 1st Weekend

Georgian Bay Poker Run 1997) **Penetanguishene** Long Weekend

Huronia Festival of Arts & Crafts **Kempenfelt** 1st Weekend

Pioneer Day **Lang Pioneer Village** 1st Weekend

Arts & Craft Show **Bobcaygeon** 1st Weekend

Annual Car & Truck Show **Fenelon Falls** Early August

Centre of Power Boat Show **Port of Orillia** 1st Weekend

Kempenfest **Barrie** 1st Weekend

Fair and Horseshow **Sutton** 1st Weekend

Horticultural Society Summer Show **Cobourg** 4th Weekend

Agricultural Fair **Campbellford** 2nd Weekend

Annual Sidewalk Sale and Car Show **Frankford** 3rd Week

Craft Show & Sale **Lindsay** Early August

Whitewater Kayak Race **Burleigh Falls** Mid August

Coby Family Games Day **Coboconk** Early August

Quinte Exhibition **Belleville** Late August

Wildlife Art Festival **Buckhorn** Mid August

Northumberland Arts, Crafts & Quilt Show **Cambellford** Mid August

Agricultural Fair **Fenelon Falls** Mid August

Arts, Crafts & Antique Show **Hastings** Early August

Top Bass Fishing Tournament **Hastings** Mid August

Annual Home & Leisure Show **Hastings** Mid August

Summerfest **Keene** Mid August

Kirkfield Festival **Kirkfield** Late August

Festival of Horses **Lakefield** Mid August

Annual Antique Show & Sale **Lakefield** Mid August

Annual Celebrations **Lang Pioneer Village** Mid August

Agricultural Fair **Lang Pioneer Village** Late August

Annual Antique Show & Sale **Orillia Square Mall** Early August

Waterfowl Festival **Orillia Square Mall** Late August

Family Fishing Derby **Campbellford** Early August

Reel Fish'n Comp. **Hastings** Mid August

Kirkfield Festival **Kirkfield** Late August

September

Pioneer Craft Day **Lang** 1st weekend

Kinmount Fair **Kinmount** Late Aug - Early September

Fall Fair **Port Perry** 1st weekend

Fall Fair **Beaverton** 2nd weekend

Quinte Agricultural Fair **Belleville** 1st weekend

Fall Boat Show **Keswick** Mid September

Festival of Conservation and Art **Midland** 3rd weekend

Central Exhibition **Lindsay** 3rd weekend

Fall Fair "The Daddy 'Em All" **Bobcaygeon** Late September

Rotary Fantasy Auction **Campbellford** Late September

Fall Fair **Coboconk**

Emerald Isle Bass Tournament **Ennismore** Mid September

Fall Fair **Orillia** Early September

Jazz Festival **Peterborough** Mid September

Annual Scottish/Irish Festival **Trenton** Mid September

Kawartha Settlers' Village Quilt Show **Bobcaygeon** Early Sept.

Victoria County Studio Tour **Victoria County** Late September

October

Cycling Club 'Tour of Rice Lake' **Cobourg** Early October

Images Studio Tour **Orillia-Barrie** Thanksgiving

Harvest Homecoming Studio Tour **Kinmount** Mid Oct.

Kawartha Autumn Studio Tour **Peterborough** Early October

Pow Wow **Rama** Thanksgiving

Annual Open House **Whetung's Ojibway Crafts & Art Gallery** Thanksgiving

Annual Close of Navigation Season **Trent-Severn Waterway** Wednesday following Thanksgiving Weekend

Note: Please check with community Chambers of Commerce and tourist information centres for exact dates and locations for special events which may change from time to time. Travel information sources and Chamber of Commerce telephone numbers can be found on the Travel Information page at the back of this guide.

Leacock Sunshine Sidewalk Sale, Downtown Orillia

Waterway Exploring

● ● ● ● ● ● ● ● ● ● ● ● ● ● ● ● ●

If you are interested in exploring the Trent-Severn Waterway but don't own a boat, it doesn't matter! There are a variety of options available to visitors who want to explore this fascinating waterway for just a few hours, a weekend or a full 5 day riverboat cruise. Sightseeing boats are strategically positioned along the Trent-Severn. Houseboat rental companies offer close to 100 vessels to choose from at various locations along the waterway corridor. Medium sized cruisers can be chosen for a great voyage of exploration offering one-way trips allowing more time to linger and an opportunity to see more of the waterway. Some boats offer dinner cruises and dancing, while others offer interesting river cruises off the main waterway channels giving visitors a different perspective of the waterway and a unique chance to view shoreline wildlife.

There's one real ship cruising the Trent-Severn. It's the 108 foot Kawartha Voyageur. It offers its 38 guests quality service during 5 day one way trips between Peterborough and Big Chute. Passengers can lounge on front and rear decks plus the huge roof top deck aboard this two level riverboat complete with private air conditioned cabins and second level dining and recreation area.

The Kawartha Voyageur at Peterborough Lift Lock

Operated by the Ackert family of Orillia, the Kawartha Voyageur offers its guests a comfortable and relaxed way to see all the sights and sounds the Trent-Severn has to offer topped off by delicious homemade meals prepared daily in the ship's galley. Each night the Kawartha Voyageur stops over at one of the Trent-Severn's many inviting and historic towns; the perfect opportunity to leave ship and explore. Anyone wanting to explore the waterway aboard the Kawartha Voyageur is advised to book well in advance as cabins are usually booked to capacity early in the cruising season. During recent ship renovations and improvements a cabin was added to meet the needs of the physically challenged plus an elevator to further ease guest mobility.

Captains and brothers Marc and John Ackert and their wonderful crew provide a unique brand of waterway hospitality for their ship-board guests and visitors who stop by to look over the Kawartha Voyageur when she's in port. Don't be shy to stop and say hello and ask for a brochure.

For those wanting to captain their own little ships a good selection of houseboats are available from charter operators in the Havelock and Rice Lake area in the south. In the popular Kawartha Lakes region there are at least three main charter companies providing houseboats up to 40-feet in length with sleeping accommodations for up to 10 passengers. Great for large family groups travelling together. For couples and honeymooners there are smaller boats available too. For those interested in exploring the northern end of the system there's a houseboat charter company based in Orillia.

Egan Marine Houseboat

The majority of houseboats come fully equipped with stoves, fridges, washrooms, showers, dishes, cooking utensils and BBQ's. Bring along bedding, groceries, toiletries, fishing gear and pack light.

For visitors interested in shorter sightseeing cruises there are a number of comfortable vessels offering this service. They are located in Campbellford, Peterborough, Lakefield, Young's Point, Stoney Lake, Fenelon Falls, Lindsay, Barrie, Orillia and Midland.

The Skylark VIII in Lindsay

Each offers a unique trip and spectacular waterway scenery.

The Lift Lock Cruises boat out of Peterborough Marina takes up to 100 passengers on a cruise over the Peterborough Lift Lock, the highest hydraulic lift lock in the world with a vertical rise of some 65 feet/17 m.

Lift Lock Cruises, Island Princess

Cruises on Stoney Lake remind visitors of the steamboat era on the waterway when cottage country was being opened at the turn of the century.

Stoney Lake offers great vistas as boats glide past some of the more than 1,000 islands that dot this huge lake and

Stoney Lake Navigation Company's, Admiral Sir John

45

its host of modern and old style summer cottages.

For those wanting to replicate travel by native and early settlers there are a number of outfitters along the waterway offering canoe rentals as well as outboard run-abouts if you're in more of a hurry.

For information on any of the above mentioned cruising opportunities contact :

Ontario Waterway Cruises -Kawartha Voyageur - Orillia	1-800-561-5767
Stoney Lake Navigation Co. - Lakefield -	(705) 652-0480
Stony Lake Cruises - Mount Julien -	(705) 654-5253
Skylark VIII Riverboat Cruises - Lindsay	(705) 324-8335
Fenelon Falls, Bobcaygeon Boat Cruises -	(705) 887-9313
Lift Lock Cruises - Peterborough	(705) 742-9912
Orillia Boat Cruises - Orillia	(705) 325-2628
30,000 Island Cruises - Midland	(705) 526-7884
Egan Marine Houseboats - Pigeon Lake	1-800-720-3426
R&R Houseboats - Chemong Lake	(705) 743-8313
Princess Houseboats - Havelock	(705) 778-7317
Gord Souter Houseboat Vacations - Orillia	(705) 327-7591
Happy Days Houseboats - Pigeon Lake	(705) 738-2201
The Boat House (Pontoon Boat Rentals) - Hastings	(705) 696-2628
Discover Ontario Adventure(Cruiser Rentals)- Lakefield	1-800-386-6097
Pulaski Boats-Adventure Fitness (Canoes)-Lakefield	(705)652-7041

Or ask area Chambers of Commerce for local cruising opportunities, numbers are available on the Tourist Infomation page at the end of this guide.

Caravelle II, Fenelon Falls

Area

1

Trenton to Healey Falls

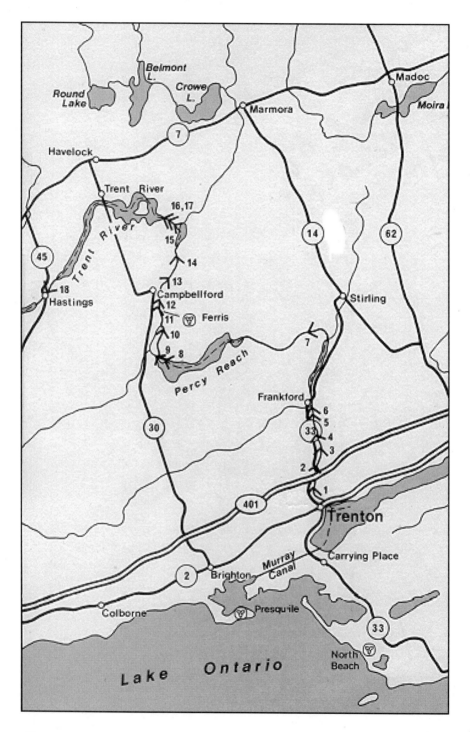

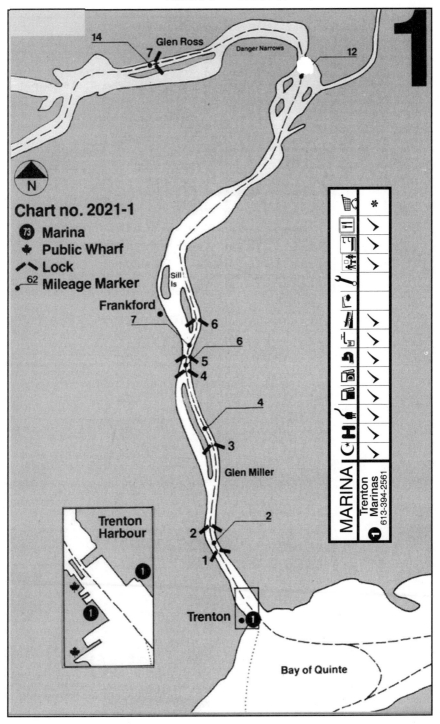

Navigation Note

As you enter the Trent-Severn Waterway, watch for strong cross currents at the first lock. Increase power and steer against current.

Fraser Park Marina, Trenton

Trenton

● ● ● ● ● ● ● ● ● ● ● ● ● ● ● ● ● ● ●

Trenton, originally called Trent Port, was first settled in 1790 by United Empire Loyalists. One of these, John Bleeker, settled on a land grant at the mouth of the Trent River. He soon established a ferry service to cross the river while his wife operated an inn. The first lumber mill was built in Trent Port in 1795. Situated halfway between Kingston and York (Toronto) and because the river supported many mills, Trent Port quickly became a prosperous village.

The Trenton area plays host to 6 of the Trent-Severn's 44 locks, and to the Murray Canal which connects the Bay of Quinte to Lake Ontario.

The Fraser Park Marina welcomes hundreds of overnight visitors each season. It is equipped with full canteen facilities, outdoor patio, additional docks, tourist information and beautiful surroundings that have been professionally landscaped for your boating enjoyment. Fraser Park is a few short steps from Trenton's Downtown shopping area. For boats entering from the United States, Fraser Park Marina is also a point from which you may contact Canada Customs. Check out the new "Lighthouse" tourist information centre adjacent to the marina.

Just about anything you might want or need can be found in Trenton, from fine dining to fast food outlets and from shopping malls to quaint little shops in which to browse. Your choice of accommodation from hotel to B & B is also available here.

Downtown Trenton has over 200 businesses ready to serve you. With many parks, and benches, it is a great place to shop, walk, visit or rest. The City of Trenton is home to Canadian Forces Base Trenton and the Rescue Co-ordination Centre for the Great Lakes Area. Trenton is the gateway to the Trent-Severn Waterway and the focal point for some of the best fishing, boating and recreation areas in central Ontario. Downtown Trenton plays host to a number of festivals each year. See the following page for details about fun summer events in Trenton. By car you can find Trenton conveniently located on Hwys 401, 2 and 33.

Scottish/ Irish Festival, Trenton

Side walk sale during annual downtown Trenton Summer Festival sponsored by Downtown Business Improvement Area (DBIA)

Quinte Bay Cloggers, Summer Festival in front of City Hall, Trenton

WELCOME TO TRENTON

THE "GATEWAY TO THE TRENT-SEVERN WATERWAY"

1997 BOATING SEASON SPECIAL EVENTS

May 3 - 4
17th Annual Kiwanis "Walleye World"
Fishing Weekend
(Trent River & Bay of Quinte)

July 1
Canada Day Celebrations
(Centennial Park - Beside Arenas)

July 4 - 6
CANATS '97
Canadian Street Rod Association
(Centennial Park - Beside Arenas)

July 17 - 20
10th Annual Summer Festival
(Centennial Park - Beside Arenas)
Flotilla of Lights & Fireworks
(Mouth of Trent River)
10th Annual Great Bathtub Race
(Bay of Quinte)

August 1 - 3
Classic Country Music Reunion
(Centennial Park - Beside Arenas)

September 13
6th Annual Scottish/Irish Festival
& Parade of Bands
(Bayshore Park)

Festivals Trenton - 16 Albert Street,
Trenton, Ontario K8V 4S3
(613) 392-3243
Contact us for information on 1998 Festivals

Trenton: Lock # 1

Many spectators arrive by car and on foot to watch operations at the Greenhorn Lock and begin a road tour on the Apple Route. It is so named because it is the first lock at the southern end of the waterway and for many boaters, it is the first lock experience. Charts and passes are available here.

There is a C.N. Railway main line just south of the lock, so you may prefer to tie up on the north side. Within a 15 minute walk of the lock, there are gas stations, a variety store and a motel and dining room.

The Friends of the Trent-Severn Waterway also operate a unique gift shop at lock 1 plus there's a Waterway interpretive centre highlighted by full size historic figures and an interactive information system.

Lock 1

Sidney: Lock # 2

This lock is visible from Highway 401 and is a convenient place for driving and cruising relatives to meet. A short walk across the dam will bring you to a motel and licensed restaurant. There are no gas or grocery facilities nearby.

The upper reach is better for tie-up because it is closer to park facilities and tends to be quieter. You might be interested in taking a tour of the local cheese factory. If so, the lockmaster can advise you on tour arrangements.

Glen Miller: Lock #3

Boats should proceed slowly into the long reach which precedes this lock because the wake creates a dangerous situation around the lock gates. Boats are not allowed to tie up at the west side of the lower reach because there is a heavy discharge of water from the emptying chamber into that area.

There is a lunch counter, grocery store and gas station a short walk from the lock. For car travellers this lock can be found on County Road 4.

Batawa: Lock #4

Located just off of Hwy 33 , the original lockmaster's house now serves as a lock office. It was recently renovated and has excellent washroom facilities. Although there are no grocery stores in the vicinity, the Bata Shoe Factory Outlet is just 10 minutes from the lock and is well worth a visit. Batawa lock is also popular with anglers who come to fish at the dam.

Trent: Lock #5

The lock office here is also the original lockmaster's house. During the 1920s and 1930s, it rented for about five dollars a month. In those days, the locks were open 24 hours a day, although there were only about 50 boats locked through all season. At night, boats were locked through by lantern.

There are no stores in this area. Boaters proceeding downstream should stay close to the centre of the channel as there is a shoal to the west side.

Frankford: Lock #6

From the lock, it is a 10 minute walk to Frankford, where there is a licensed restaurant. A gas station, grocery store and restaurant are nearby on the east side of the lock.

The tie-ups upstream of the lock are closer to the town and to the fresh water available at the trailer camp.

Frankford

● ● ● ● ● ● ● ● ● ● ● ● ● ● ● ● ● ●

Known as "the Wild Turkey Capital of Ontario", Frankford is situated where the tributary Cold Creek empties into the Trent. This village offers an interesting stopover for boaters. Prior to construction of the Trent Canal System the area was known as the last safe point to ford the river before the 9 miles/14.5 km of rapids extending downstream to Trenton.

Although the embankment separating the raised canal from the river denies a good view of the surroundings, boaters that moor at the locks, and set off by foot or bike, can explore the quaint and picturesque village close by. Between the canal and the river lies a municipal tourist park with picnic, beach, and playground facilities. Sights from the top of the bridge may include the large flocks of Canada Geese which reside year round, a nesting osprey (check atop the nearby hydro pole), large carp in the shallow waters below, and Dam 6 just upstream. There are many services and attractions within walking distance such as: the Orville Berry Museum featuring extensive displays of early household items, glassworks and military memorabilia. Shopping, coin laundry, beer and liquor store, restaurants, post office, and 6 churches can be found here. As well there is a challenging 9 hole municipal golf course straddling Cold Creek and camping nearby.

Upstream—The 7 mile/11 km stretch above Frankford is a most scenic section where the rolling hills of the Trent valley hug the river on both sides. Pike, pickerel, bass, and muskellunge fishing may be enjoyed. Keep an eye out along the east bank for sightings of Wild Turkeys.

aerial view of Frankford Dam

Glen Ross: Lock #7

Glen Ross has been nicknamed the Flower Lock because of the beds of beautiful blossoms around the lock. Although you don't have to stop and smell the roses, you are advised to enter the lock channel very slowly. The force of waves and back-wash in this narrow channel can push the lock gates hard enough to spin the sweeps and cause injury to the lock staff.

A swing bridge is immediately upstream of the lock and it is difficult for staff to see boats approaching the bridge. Three toots of your horn will alert staff of your approach. The tie-up area downstream is provided with picnic tables and there is a small store by the lock which carries groceries, snacks and bait.

Percy Reach: Lock #8

The popularity of this lock could be due to many factors. One of these could be the excellent bass and pickerel fishing downstream of the lock gates. The prevailing winds are usually from the west, so watch for the flag and steer accordingly.

Centennial Hiking Trail connects lock 8 and lock 9 along the west side of the canal. This is a 1.5 mile/2.4 km trail, keep your eyes and ears open, this is a great spot for birding. Murray Marsh can be seen on approach on either side, this is an extremely diverse environmental attraction for naturalists.

Meyers: Lock #9

This is a peaceful lock surrounded by spacious parkland. If you find it too windy at Hagues Reach, you might prefer to tie up downstream from the lock. There are no stores in the vicinity.

The original lockmaster's house was built between 1915 and 1920 when it cost 35 cents for a boat trip from Campbellford to Percy Reach on river boat cruises.

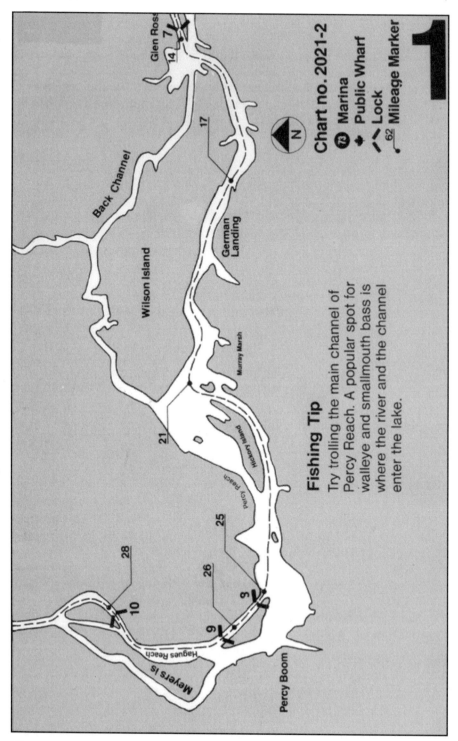

Fishing Tip

Try trolling the main channel of Percy Reach. A popular spot for walleye and smallmouth bass is where the river and the channel enter the lake.

Chart no. 2021-2

🅜 Marina
⚓ Public Wharf
∧ Lock
•⁶² Mileage Marker

N

Glen Ross
14 7

Back Channel

Wilson Island

German Landing

17

Murray Marsh

21

Hickory Island

Percy Reach

25

26

28

10

9

Hagues Reach

Meyers Is

Percy Boom

Hagues Reach: Lock #10

Another secluded and quiet lock, this has excellent tie-up space and washroom facilities. It is recommended that you tie up on the east wall, because the water discharge from the lock chamber can create a lot of turbulence.

Ranney Falls:Lock #11 & #12

Be forewarned - the strong whirlpool at the swing bridge upstream can be dangerous for small craft. Please exercise caution. Also, use your horn when coming through the swing bridge to alert lock staff of your approach. Boats are marshalled over a P.A. system into these 2 locks which move boats up and down simultaneously.

The tie-up upstream is closer to town which is a walk of approximately 1 mile/1.6 kms. Parkland runs from the lock right into Campbellford. Both residents and visitors often enjoy a healthy stroll along the Rotary trail circuit beside the river.

Ferris Provincial Park is just 1.25 miles/2 kms south of Campbellford. This park offers some great woodland trails and drumlins for you to explore. For information call (705) 866-0530.

Chart no. 2021-3

MARINA	☾	H	⛽	gas	diesel	anchor	glass	laundry	buoy	wrench	picnic	bed	🍴	cart
Old Mill Park 705-653-1551	✓	✓	✓	✻	✻	✻	✓	✓		✓	✓			✻
Campbellford River Inn 705-653-1771	✓		✓											✓
Sandy Bay Cottages 705-696-2951	✓		✓	✓		✓	✓		✓	✓	✓			✓

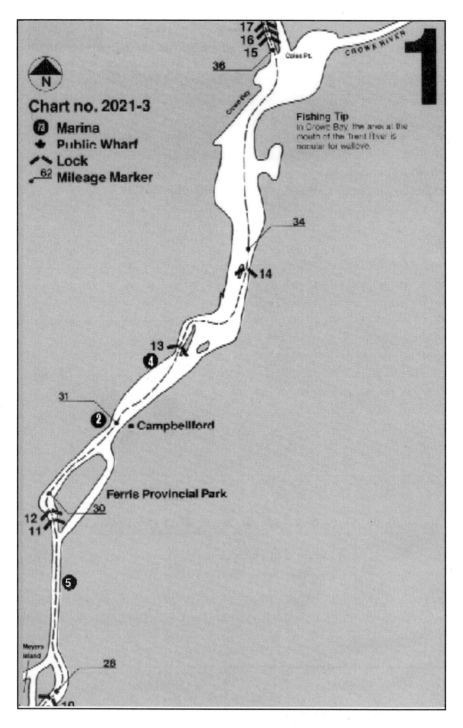

Chart no. 2021-3

🅝 Marina
⚓ Public Wharf
✂ Lock
62 Mileage Marker

CROWE RIVER

Coles Pt.

Crowe Bay

Fishing Tip
In Crowe Bay, the area at the mouth of the Trent River is popular for walleye.

Campbellford

Ferris Provincial Park

Meyers Island

Campbellford

T his site was originally known as Campbell's Ford, where the Campbell brothers were given a land grant. Lt. Col. Robert Campbell and Major David Campbell had served in the Napoleonic Wars and resettled in Upper Canada when the wars ended. The success of the lumber business had a strong effect on Campbellford and in 1876 it was incorporated as a village.

With lumbering days long gone, Campbellford today is in the heart of dairy farming country. There are cheese and chocolate factories in town, so it is a good opportunity to stock up on both.

The town has marinas, dozens of stores, many restaurants and tea rooms, grocery stores, Campbellford River Inn with docking facilities, as well as B&B accommodations, and laundromats. There is a lovely evening lit park, where the Chamber of Commerce visitor information centre is located just south of the bridge. "Old Mill Park" provides dockage with shore power and access to showers and washrooms. A pumpout and 2 fuel locations are available nearby.

The traditional Canada week celebrations feature: Treats in the Streets, a Jamboree, entertainment in the park, Heritage tours, and it all starts the last week in June. The usual date of the Campbellford Antique Show and Sale is the second weekend in July. Rotary's Golf Tournament is the 1st Thursday of August. The Campbellford-Seymour Agricultural Fair is held the 1st weekend after the Civic holiday. The successful Campbellford Trade show and the amazing Touch of Country Decor craft show are held the 3rd weekend of September and the Campbellford Jamboree is held the fourth Saturday of each month. An active Farmer's Market runs from May through September. Campbellford can be found on Hwy 30; it is intersected by County Rds. 8, 38, 50 and 35.

Campbellford Town Dock and Old Mill Park

Campbellford: Lock #13

A drawing feature of this lock is good, thirst-quenching well water. There is a popular swimming area upstream from the lock and Campbellford is just 1 mile/1.6 kms south. Watch for Osprey in this area.

Crowe Bay: Lock #14

This quiet lock, bordered with spacious parkland, has good pickerel/walleye fishing around the powerhouse. The tie-up area upstream from the lock is closer to the parkland. The Crowe River flows into the Trent approximately 2 miles upriver.

Campbellford heading toward Hastings

Healey Falls: Lock #15

When proceeding upstream, you can help speed up the lock process by keeping to port side. In this formation, only the hydraulic valve has to be opened, thus speeding up lockage. When boats are on both sides of the lock, the manual valves must be used and that results in slower lockage.

There is a basin just north and west which has good tie-up space surrounded by parkland. The lockmaster suggests you do not tie up to the starboard wall of the lower side of the lock due to a very strong current when the lock is emptied. Most facilities are on the upper level anyway. County Road 37 will get you there by car.

Healey Falls: Locks #16 & #17

These flight locks have a total drop of 54 feet/16.5 m. It takes approximately 45 minutes to go through the locks. There is no overnight tie-up at the downstream area of the locks, but you can tie up on the west wall upstream. There are no stores in the vicinity but it is worthwhile tying up and taking time for the 15 minute jaunt to Healey Falls. It is a beautiful sight and one which photography buffs will want to capture. The fishing is very good around the powerhouse.

A Circle Tour of Northumberland

● ● ● ● ● ● ● ● ● ● ● ● ● ● ● ● ● ● ● ●

Dock your boat at Old Mill Park in Campbellford, along the wall in Hastings or at any of the marinas along the way. Now you are ready for a landlubber's adventure.

In Campbellford, don't miss the Canadian Military Museum and Prototype Research Replicars. The museum began as a childhood hobby of collecting model airplanes. It outgrew the basement and the garage. Now real planes surround this collection of military memorabilia. Across the way is the finest collection of new-old cars that you are likely to see. At Prototype research some of the finest old model cars are reproduced with modern materials. You won't want to leave without at least a do-it-yourself kit!

For the gardener, Roy's Rose Garden is rose heaven. Over in Warkworth, Schoolhouse Gardens is a herb lovers delight. Dennis and Tom are passionate about herbs. Enjoy a tour of the garden, tea and don't miss out on some of their creations.

In Hastings, you can take a walking tour of the many fine historical homes in the village. Pick up a guide at the town hall. Down Highway 45 from Hastings, you'll discover the Roseneath Carousel, lovingly restored, and if you're lucky you may get a ride. Further south, is the Northumberland County forest, where trails beckon the hiker or biker.

Then on down to Cobourg, where a lunch stop would be in order. There are a variety of restaurants to choose from, fast food to fine dining. Visit Cobourg's marina and harbour for a swim at the beach or a picnic.

Head east of Cobourg on Highway 2 to Grafton. A sprinkling of antique shops and the Barnum House Museum await you. Built in the early 1800s by Eliakim Barnum, it is one of the finest examples of neo-classic architecture in Canada. Further east of #2 you will encounter The Apple Route and its many road side fruit stands.

Just north of Colborne you will find Hoselton Studio and its family made aluminum and marble statues, famous around the globe. In Brighton you must make the trip to Presqu'ile Park and its beautiful beaches, great birding, marsh boardwalk, camping, hiking, and more. North on Highway 30 will take you back to Campbellford.

The Three R's...
relax, refresh, rejuvenate.

It's one of those well-kept secrets. Leave your stress behind, and head for Northumberland to relax, refresh and rejuvenate. Grab a fishing pole, cruise the Trent-Severn Waterway or travel country roads to the nearest auction or flea market. The living is easy... in Northumberland County - Holiday Our Way. For your FREE copy of the Northumberland County travel guide, please call:

Northumberland County Tourism
1-800-354-7050 x-237

County of Northumberland Tourism
860 William St., Cobourg, Ontario K9A 3A9
Website: www.eagle.ca/tourism • e-mail: tourism@eagle.ca

Travel Notes

· · · · · · · · · · · · · · · ·

aerial view of lock 10

Area

2

Healey
Falls
to
Peterborough

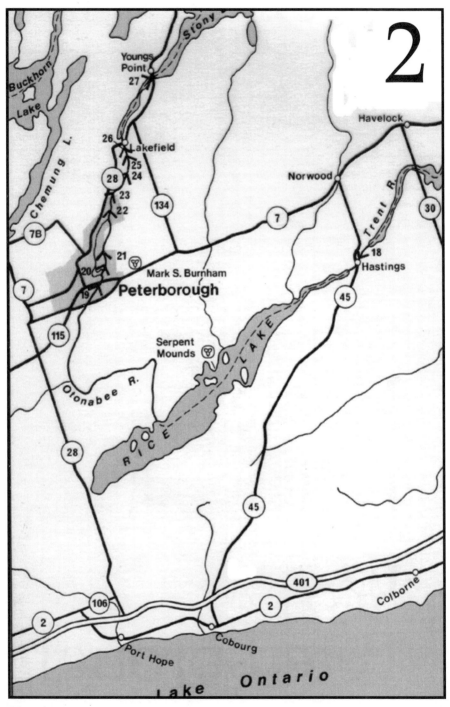

2

Buckhorn Lake

Chemung L.

Stony

Youngs Point
27

26
Lakefield
25
28 24
23
22

134

7B

21

7

20
19

Mark S. Burnham

Peterborough

115

Serpent Mounds

Otonabee R.

28

R I C E

L A K E

Havelock

Norwood

Trent R.

30

18
Hastings

45

7

45

45

401

106

2

2

Colborne

Port Hope

Cobourg

Lake   Ontario

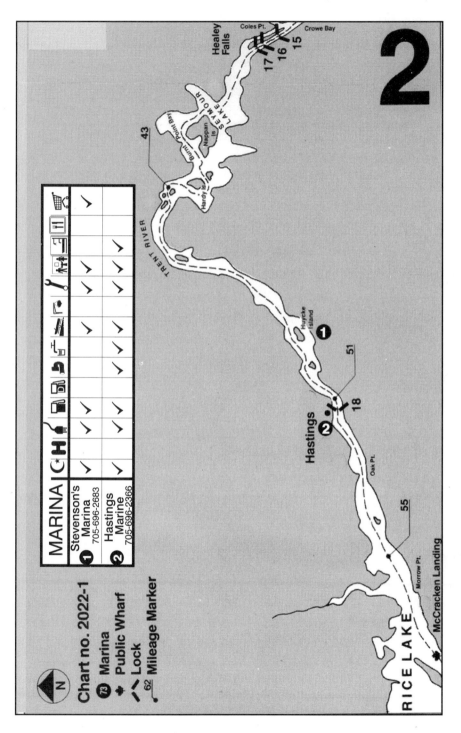

Hastings Lock #18

Hastings: Lock #18

The Old Mill on the downstream side of this lock used to be a casting foundry where cast iron stoves were made. It was built in the 1800s and was operated by water power.

There is plenty of tie-up space at the lock which is located right in town close to grocery, beer and liquor stores. The upstream tie-ups have easier access to the town while those tie-ups downstream are closer to the washrooms.

If you are interested in pickerel/walleye and bass, angling is popular along the lock walls and the dam.

Chart no. 2022-2

MARINA	☾	H	🔌	⛽	🛢	⚓	🚿	🛥	🪝	🔧	🚻	🛏	🍴	🛒
❸ Elmhirst Resort 705-295-4591	✓		✓	✓		✓	✓						✓	✓
❹ Cox'ies Cove 905-342-2138	✓	✓	✓	✓		✓	✓	✓	✓	✓	✓	✓	✓	❇
❺ Harris Boat Works 905-342-2153	✓	✓	✓	✓		✓	✓	✓	✓	✓	✓			
❻ Heartland Marina 705-797-2790	✓		✓	✓		✓	✓			✓	✓	✓		
❼ Sandercocks Tourist Resort 905-352-2469	✓			✓		✓	✓				✓	✓	✓	✓

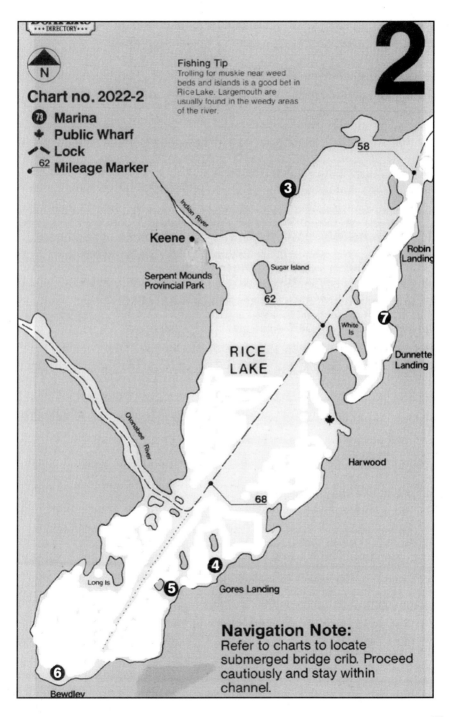

2

Chart no. 2022-2

🅱 Marina
⚜ Public Wharf
➤ Lock
•⁶² Mileage Marker

Fishing Tip
Trolling for muskie near weed beds and islands is a good bet in Rice Lake. Largemouth are usually found in the weedy areas of the river.

58

3

Indian River

Keene •

Robin Landing

Serpent Mounds Provincial Park

Sugar Island

62

White Is

7

Dunnette Landing

RICE LAKE

Otonabee River

Harwood

68

4

Long Is

5

Gores Landing

6

Bewdley

Navigation Note:
Refer to charts to locate submerged bridge crib. Proceed cautiously and stay within channel.

Hastings

●●●●●●●●●●●●●●●●●●●

The quaint village of Hastings is located 14 miles/20 kms upriver from Healey Falls. Lock 18 in the centre of this community will lift you 9 feet/2.75 m higher on the Trent River where you will be able to cruise the final 6 miles/9.6 kms along the widening river into Rice Lake. Hastings is known as the "hub of the Trent". Originally named Crook's Rapids, Hastings is the location of the first dam constructed in 1838 for the Trent Canal System. Here there is good tie up space above the lock affording waterway visitors an opportunity to explore this interesting centre which provides a variety of shopping and entertainment opportunities.

Just up from the main east-west shopping area is a good food liner offering a full line of provisions. There are a number of restaurants just steps from the lock wall as well as beer and liquor stores. Hastings enjoys an excellent waterfront setting with expansive parks lining both sides of the waterway right through town. There is also a nice little public beach just upstream from the docking area.

For boaters requiring any marine services Hastings Marine is upstream on the right side. Docking is available with power, fuel and pumpout service, along with a launch ramp. The Hastings Chamber of Commerce is actively working on a significant waterfront marina development plan which hopefully in the next few years will offer full docking service to transient and seasonal boaters in this active boating centre.

On the right just before entering the Hastings lock is the site of the new Osprey Point-on-the-Trent Adult Lifestyle Condominium Project which is currently under development. Hastings' ideal location in terms of water and road access make this community an ideal retirement place. Every recreational amenity is at hand. Great fishing, boating, golf plus theatre, galleries and good shopping and dining are at the door step. Take a few minutes from your cruising schedule and explore the town. Osprey Point condominium models are open for viewing. The site is extraordinary in that it fronts on the Trent-Severn and the balance of the property is on the historic mill pond with the 1871 stone mill still standing in the background. Just imagine being able to design the interior of your Victorian style condo home, signing up for your free golf membership and booking your boat dock all at the same time.

picnic on Rice Lake

Harwood

●●●●●●●●●●●●●●●●●●

This scenic village was first a tract of land owned by Robert Harwood who bought it in 1828. The land began to develop when the Cobourg and Peterborough railway was built in the 1850s. It was from here that a railway line supported on a crib-bridge was built across Rice Lake to transport passengers and goods between Peterborough and Lake Ontario towns. The bridge was poorly constructed and because of extensive damage by ice break-up had to be closed in 1862. The line from Harwood to Cobourg became a well established point of trans-shipment for lumber. Once the timber was gone the sawmill and railroads folded and Harwood, like many lakeshore villages, became a tourist centre.

Remains of the bridge cribs still lie across Rice Lake and it is important to stay in the channel here or you may lose a prop.

Harwood is primarily a resort community today and has a number of marinas, accommodation and restaurants. It is located at the junction of County Roads 18 and 15. Nearby is the Harwood Fish Culture Station operated by the Ministry of Natural Resources. There is a self-guided visitor centre with aquarium and video on fish culture. Call (905) 342-2860 for information.

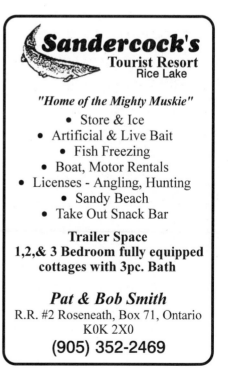

Gore's Landing

●●●●●●●●●●●●●●●●●●

G ore's Landing village was a choice location for settlement due
to its high location and excellent fishing and hunting. In 1846
surveyor Thomas Gore built a road, partially made of planks, connecting the village to Cobourg. This road became known as 'the old
plank road' and made a significant impact, cutting the travel time from
Cobourg to an hour and a half, from an uncomfortable day.

Gore's Landing is noted for its double-verandah frame houses and
has always been a mecca for artists and writers. On the government
dock you will find a gazebo, originally designed by artist Gerald
Hayward. Nearby be sure to visit one of the prettiest Anglican churches in Ontario, St. George's-on-the-hill.

At Gore's Landing you can dock at Cox'ies Cove Marina and take
in the beauty of the area and stay for a great meal or a comfortable
night at Victoria Inn. It was originally named 'The Willows', built in
1902 as the summer home of Gerald Hayward.

aerial view of Gore's Landing & Rice Lake

Victoria Inn

Elmhirst's Resort, Rice Lake

Keene

●●●●●●●●●●●●●●●●●●

B oats heading into Indian River should proceed with caution, as depths in this area are very shallow. Refer to marine chart for depths.

The small village of Keene is on the Indian River, just north of Rice Lake. There is a restaurant and a tea room in the village, a general store, bank, an art gallery and several quaint gift shops. Two miles from Keene is Lang Pioneer Village. Keene is located at the intersection of County Roads 2 and 34.

Serpent Mounds Provincial Park

●●●●●●●●●●●●●●●●●●

O n the north shore of Rice Lake, at Roach Point, you'll find the Serpent Mounds Provincial Park. Archaeological evidence shows that native people gathered at this site over 2,000 years ago.

At the top of the hill, near a stand of oak trees, are 9 burial mounds. Eight have an ovate shape, much like others discovered throughout Ontario. The 9th, however, measures 190 feet/58 m by approximately 30 feet/9 m and is angled in a zig-zag fashion so that it resembles a snake. This "Serpent Mound" is unique in Canada. The shape is an enigma to archaeologists and tourists alike.

Near the Serpent Mounds is an interpretive building and an outdoor theatre where evening programs are presented on a weekly basis. As well as having a playground for children, the park has 3 beaches, one of which has a boat rental outlet. There are 2 boat launching ramps and a small floating wharf. Serpent Mounds has campsites, but no electricity. Campsites are equipped with fireplaces and picnic tables. The comfort stations have showers and laundry facilities. A store and restaurant are located near the park entrance. For details call (705) 295-6879.

Lang Pioneer Village

●●●●●●●●●●●●●●●●

No vacation to the Kawarthas is complete without a visit to LANG PIONEER VILLAGE

Nestled along the banks of the Indian River, just north of the scenic Village of Keene, Lang Pioneer Village is home to over 20 restored, historic buildings from the early days of Peterborough County. Representing the rigors of pioneer life from 1800 to 1900, friendly, costumed interpreters take time out from their daily chores of gardening, baking and tending the animals to welcome you to their homes. Spend the day visiting in the general store, watching sparks fly in the blacksmith shop, smelling the fresh wood shavings in the carpenter shop, or admiring the wares in the tinshop. Refresh yourself from your day of visiting with a glass of lemonade in the 14 room Keene Hotel, restored to its former glory of the 1870s.

Lang Pioneer Village, a photographer's paradise, was established by the County of Peterborough in 1967 to preserve the unique history of the area. Since that time thousands of visitors from around the world have taken the trip back in time to experience a simpler life.

While the historic buildings at Lang Pioneer Village are open from late May to Labour Day, the interpretation Centre and Administration Buildings are open, and available for research and staff are on-site to answer questions, year round. The Interpretive Centre houses a museum exhibit gallery, visitor reception area, a multipurpose room- available for meetings, as well as environmentally controlled facilities for archives, artifact storage, a conservation laboratory, and other work

Fife House - Lang Pioneer Village

areas. The Gift Shop is also housed in the Interpretation Centre, it specializes in both local and hand-crafted Village-made wares.

Don't miss Lang Pioneer Village Special Event Days! In addition to their regular daily activities and demonstrations, Special Event Days focus on a special theme. There is everything from Canada Day, County Fair Day, and Canoe Day, to Antique Tractor and Steam Day, plus a War of 1812 Re-Enactment! There's always something Going On! Call the village for a complete up-to-date list of special events and their dates!

Lang Pioneer Village, is situated on a 25 acre site between two restored, historic water-powered mills. Included with admission to Lang Pioneer Village is the opportunity to visit the Lang Grist Mill where interpreters demonstrate the 1896 roller-mill technique for producing whole wheat flour, which is also available for sale.

To get to Lang take Highway 7 for 7 miles/10 kms east of Peterborough, then south on County Road 34 for 4 miles/6 kms. Turn east(left) at the sign into the Village of Lang. The Museum entrance is just past the mill on the left. From County Road 2 it is 2miles/3.5 kms

Fitzpatrick House - Lang Pioneer Village

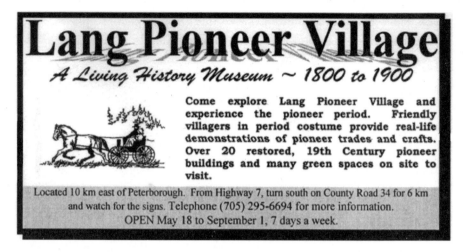

Lang Pioneer Village

A Living History Museum ~ 1800 to 1900

Come explore Lang Pioneer Village and experience the pioneer period. Friendly villagers in period costume provide real-life demonstrations of pioneer trades and crafts. Over 20 restored, 19th Century pioneer buildings and many green spaces on site to visit.

Located 10 km east of Peterborough. From Highway 7, turn south on County Road 34 for 6 km and watch for the signs. Telephone (705) 295-6694 for more information.
OPEN May 18 to September 1, 7 days a week.

North of Keene on County Road 34. **Group and Special Tours are welcome.**

Lang Pioneer Village is open 7 days a week from late May to September, call for admission prices and daily hours (705)295-6694. Treat your self to a visit to Peterborough County's only Living History Site!

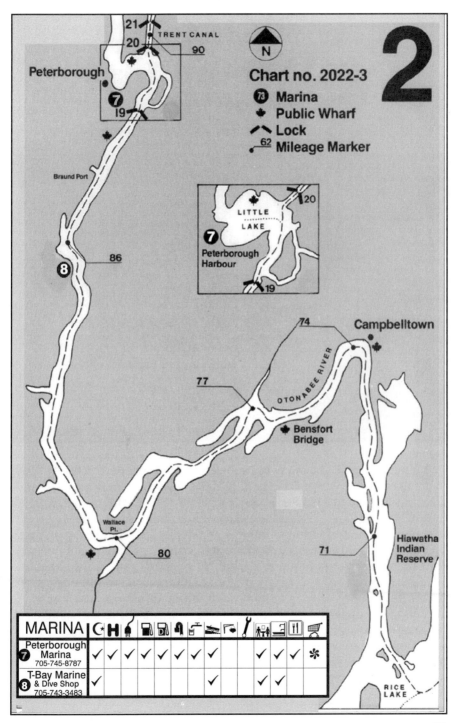

Peterborough

TRENT CANAL

21
20
90
19

Chart no. 2022-3

Marina
Public Wharf
Lock
Mileage Marker

Braund Port

86

8

LITTLE LAKE

20

Peterborough Harbour

19

74   Campbelltown

77

OTONABEE RIVER

Bensfort Bridge

Wallace Pt.

80

71

Hiawatha Indian Reserve

RICE LAKE

MARINA	C	H	⚓	⬛	⛽	🔌	🛏	🔧	⚓	🔧	🏨	🛏	🍴	🛒
7 Peterborough Marina 705-745-8787	✓	✓	✓	✓	✓	✓	✓	✓			✓	✓	✓	✳
8 T-Bay Marine & Dive Shop 705-743-3483	✓						✓				✓	✓		

Come Shore
PETERBOROUGH
the Magic!

Peterborough Marina is located right downtown in Del Crary Park home of the annual Festival Of Lights summer concert program and beside the waterfront Holiday Inn. This 100 slip marina on Little Lake between locks 19 and 20 offers visiting boaters excellent overnight docking facilities plus gas and diesel fuel, pumpout, private boater washrooms/showers, dockside restaurant, gift shop and friendly staff to guide visitors to the full array of shopping and dining experiences located close to the harbour. Peterborough and neighbouring Kawartha Country offer a number of significant heritage and fun attractions to explore. Arrangements can be made for rental vehicles at the marina for side trips. Peterborough Marina and the Holiday Inn work together to ensure boaters enjoy their stay at this close to mid-point stopover on the waterway. The Holiday Inn extends pool and fitness centre privileges to marina guests as part of the Peterborough Marina/Holiday Inn VIP Boater Program including discounts on rooms for boaters who want an evening ashore or who have guests joining them who cannot be accommodated onboard. Peterborough Marina is also home to two water ski clubs who will take boaters or their children for rides and the Lift Lock Cruise Boat that takes passengers on regular sightseeing trips up the canal and over the Lift Lock. The marina and Little Lake is also host to a variety of summer waterfront events including the annual In Water Boat Show the second weekend of August. A small boat rental centre with canoes and pedal boats is also available for anyone wanting to explore the lake and Otonabee River or perhaps drop a line for one of the elusive giant Muskie that call Little Lake home. For docking reservations call (705) 745-8787. A water taxi service is also available by calling (705)748-4774 The marina is located directly across Little Lake from Beavermead Park and Campground.

Navigation Note: The Crescent Street Wharf identified on charts as a public wharf is managed by the City of Peterborough Marina and overnight docking fees apply. Boaters are urged to check into the marina office before tying up for the night. Day use is free of charge.

Peterborough

● ● ● ● ● ● ● ● ● ● ● ● ● ● ● ● ● ●

This quickly growing city, with a population of about 68,000, has good cause for civic pride. Situated on the Otonabee River, it is the site of the world's highest Hydraulic Lift Lock (65 ft./20 m). The area was originally called Scott's Plains, after Adam Scott of Edinburgh, who settled here in 1819 and established a lumber mill and distillery. Six years later, over 2,000 Irish immigrants led by Peter Robinson made Scott's Plains their home and the town's name was eventually changed to Peterborough.

Centennial Fountain at Little Lake

In the centre of town is Little Lake and Del Crary Park, the focus of which is Centennial Fountain jetting 250 feet into the air. The Festival of Lights, which is underway from mid-June to mid-August on Little Lake, features fireworks displays and free outdoor concerts.

A short walk from the marina docks, in the heart of downtown under the town clock, lies Peterborough Square, an enclosed shopping centre. There are also numerous art galleries, museums and historical points of interest in the city. Among these is Hutchison House, a lovely stone home built in 1837 by the townspeople for Dr. John Hutchinson and his growing family; the town's hope was to convince the Doctor to stay and become the permanent resident physician. They stayed as valued and well respected members of the pioneer community until his untimely death in 1847. Dr. Hutchinson's young cousin, Sandford Fleming, also lived here in the mid 1840s while establishing himself in Upper Canada. He was an extraordinary person who accomplished great things in his long and fascinating life; Fleming's vision, surveying and engineering skills, made the construction of the Canadian Pacific Railway a reality. He designed the first Canadian Postage stamp and was primarily responsible for developing International Standard Time and the twenty-four hour clock. Hutchison House is open to the public Tuesday - Sunday 1-5 p.m.;

you will enjoy tours of the house and gardens with costumed guides, hearth cooking demonstrations and Scottish Tea (a special treat) is served daily in summer. So come for a visit to Hutchinson House, where the past still lives and speaks to the present. The museum is located at 270 Brock st., very close to the downtown area.

You can visit the Art Gallery, on Crescent Street at Little Lake, and the Peterborough Centennial Museum and Archives, on Hunter Street. The Riverview Park & Zoo offers a great outing and features a wonderful playground for children. The MacKenzie Gallery is found at Trent University, just steps away from lock 22. The Canadian Canoe Museum, located at 910 Monaghan Road, a short walk from Peterborough Marina, features the largest and best collection of canoes and kayaks in the world. Showplace Peterborough is a new and exciting community performance centre located right downtown at 290 George St. It offers a venue for all kinds of entertainment. Phone the box office at (705) 742-7089 for schedules and tickets.

If you'd like to stock up on fresh produce, Peterborough's Farmers' Market operates on Saturday until noon at Morrow Park.

Before going anywhere, it would be worthwhile to pay a visit to the Friends of the Trent-Severn Waterway. Located at the Liftlock Visitor Centre, the FTSW. is a charitable organization and its aim is to support Parks Canada in promoting awareness of the Waterway. The Friends assist with special events and give support to waterway projects. Their sales outlet, the Nautical Nook, carries many publications and other items related to the waterway. Ask about memberships or send in the form located near the end of this guide.

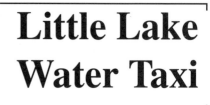

Scott's Mills: Lock #19

The original limestone blocks on the sides of the lock still stand and, as you may imagine, have witnessed quite a change in boats and fashions over the years. There is more parkland on the downstream side of the lock, so you may find it preferable to tie up there. From the lock, it is only a 5 minute walk to local stores and gas stations.

Ashburnham: Lock #20

Nicknamed 'the Forgotten Lock' because of its proximity to the Lift Lock, it still services a lot of boaters. The swing bridge upstream, which is operated by the lock staff, is heavily trafficked. If you happen through the lock about noon, you may hear references about a 'boater sandwich'. It seems that whenever lunchtime rolls around for the lock staff, another boater is ready to lock through.

The downstream reach is the best tie-up and can accommodate 10 to 15 boats. From here, it is a 15 minute walk to downtown.

Peterborough Lift Lock #21

The Peterborough Lift Lock is the highest of its kind in the world and a major visitor attraction of the Waterway. The Visitor Centre features displays about the construction and operation of the lift lock and general exhibits about the system. Films and slide presentations are shown regularly in the Theatre. The Friends of the Trent-Severn Waterway operate a gift shop featuring books, nautical charts and gift items related to the Waterway.

Boaters wishing to visit the centre may make use of the new tie-up wall on the west side of the lower reach. Overnight tie-up is only permitted above the lift lock. A short walk along Hunter Street will take you to grocery stores, shops and restaurants.

Boaters should be aware of the whale boards which run along the sides of the chamber. When the chamber takes on an extra foot of water, boats sometimes get caught on the board. To avoid this, keep your lines a bit slack and push the boat off the wall with a fender or pike pole.

docks at Peterborough Marina

Peterborough Lift Lock

The History of the Trent-Severn Waterway

●●●●●●●●●●●●●●●●●●●

The construction of the Trent-Severn Waterway has had a very sporadic history. Unlike the Rideau, which was built of political necessity and was funded by the British Government, the Trent-Severn developed slowly and painstakingly with many interruptions. In duration, its construction was spanned from the sponsorship of the Imperial Government to the Federal Government of the Dominion of Canada. Various projects, in fits and starts, resulted in the completion of the entire waterway in just over 80 years. The growth of the fur trade gave rise to a number of camps and milltowns along the inland waters. Mill construction and operation provided employment to new settlers and, for this reason, many were attracted to the new settlements. Soon, support services such as general stores, blacksmiths and inns prospered at these sites. As southern timber stands were depleted, the lumber trade pushed farther north and west along the waterways.

The 1850s were boom years for the timber trade. Large American markets were more easily accessible due to improved rail service and river transport. The waterway towns prospered and grew. By 1860, the push north had reached Port Severn, but the gradual rape of the land eventually resulted in depleted timber stands and the logging industry, more or less, put itself out of business by the turn of the century.

Interest in an inland water route to Lake Huron from Lake Ontario began as early as 1785. The overland trek from York (Toronto) to Lake Simcoe was slow and arduous. After preliminary and incomplete surveys were made, it was proposed that connecting the lakes and rivers to form a continuous water route was not feasible. The settlers and owners of timber enterprises did not agree. They petitioned for a direct water route to Lake Ontario so that supply ships and lumber rafts and barges could proceed quickly and inexpensively to larger commercial centres.

Finally in 1833, the Imperial Government sanctioned a bill to survey a route and construct locks, dams and canals at chosen sites. Civil engineer, Nicol H. Baird was appointed by Sir John Colborne to undertake the project. Baird carried out surveys from Lake Ontario to Rice Lake and from Rice Lake to Lake Simcoe and estimated the works to create a waterway would cost 2.5 million dollars. His results were approved and the project was allotted monies to start construction. The first lock sites were Bobcaygeon and Purdy's Mills, now Lindsay. This allowed navigation from Chemong, Buckhorn and Pigeon lakes into Lindsay via Sturgeon Lake and the Scugog River. Bobcaygeon lock was the first completed in 1835. A channel was dredged at Trenton and lock construction began at Hastings, Glen Ross and Peterborough.

Having done this much, a cash shortage was experienced by the Inland Water Commission and work was stopped. Attention focused instead on the 1837 Rebellion and the Inland Water Commission project became a secondary concern.

As the Rebellion threat died down, it appeared that government enthusiasm for the waterway died with it. Arguments against the waterway were that the project had too many locks to be useful or expedient anyway. It was finally agreed that those locks which had been begun, would be completed, but that the proposed lock sites would be equipped with timber slides instead. The locks which were completed, served their localized communities. Steamship cruises through a lock became a very popular vacation pastime.

In 1841, Upper Canada and Lower Canada were joined to form the Province of Canada. Further works on the waterway were transferred from the Inland Water Commission to the Boards of Works. Work was resumed on unfinished locks under the Board of Works, because it provided a means of employing the new waves of immigrants.

It wasn't until after Confederation that the provincial government built locks at Young's Point and Rosedale and a new lock was constructed at Lindsay. These were localized improvements which were not undertaken with a view to the overall waterway.

In 1879, interest in a waterway from Lake Ontario to Georgian Bay was rekindled. Sir John A. McDonald's government took over the project and made yet another survey. Locks were completed at Burleigh Falls, Lovesick Lake, Buckhorn and Fenelon Falls. These locks, together with the previously constructed locks allowed through-navigation from Lakefield to Balsam Lake. At this point, interest once again flagged. Further plans for the completion of the waterway were put aside for several years. By 1890, the Murray Canal had been cut through Presqu'ile and this helped to push the idea of an inland waterway to Georgian Bay to the fore again.

Bids were taken from contractors for 3 additional sections of locks and canals to be built. They were Trenton to Rice Lake, Peterborough to Lakefield and from Balsam Lake to Lake Simcoe. The works on these sections were completed in 1918, 1904 and 1906 respectively. The section from Lake Couchiching to Georgian Bay was completed in 1920 and consisted of locks at Washago and Port Severn and marine railways at Swift Rapids and Big Chute. It might have been completed earlier if not for the interruption of World War I. The marine railway at Swift Rapids was replaced by a large lock in 1964. Also since then, a new and larger marine railway has been built at Big Chute.

In July of 1920, the first vessel to complete a through-passage was the motor launch *Irene*. The journey from Trenton to Port Severn took nine days.

The Trent-Severn Waterway was never used for commercial traffic as originally planned. By the time it was completed, the canal draughts and lock chambers were somewhat short of modern commercial vessels. Also, rail and road transport had much improved and was a popular alternative.

Because the Waterway was completed in the not so distant past, it may be hard to realize that it was started over 160 years ago. The spirit behind the idea of an inland water route to Lake Ontario and Georgian Bay was in the heart of every waterway settler and could not help but affect their lives. Many settlers, new to Canada, found themselves gainfully employed in the hard, gruelling labour of canal digging and blasting operations.

In spite of many initial apprehensions, delays and interruptions, the Trent-Severn Waterway has become a major success. Today it is one of the primary recreational attractions in central Ontario. Thousands of boaters and motorists visit the Waterway and its corridor each year to enjoy unrivaled fishing, cruising and scenery.

How Locks Work

•••••••••••••••••••

Conventional Locks

There are 44 locks altogether, on the Trent-Severn Waterway. The majority of these are conventional chamber locks, which are used to raise and lower boats only a short distance. These locks operate on a fairly simple principle; water will always find its own level.

When a boat enters a lock, the gate closes behind it so that the boat is enclosed on all sides. This enclosure is called a chamber. Valves are contained within the walls and gates of the chamber which can be opened or closed, allowing water to enter the chamber from upriver or leave the chamber and flow downriver.

If a boat is travelling upriver, the valves upriver are opened until the water level within the chamber rises and finally equals the elevation of the water upriver. The upriver lock gates are then opened and the boat departs. When a boat travelling downriver enters the lock, the upriver gates close and the downriver valves are opened. This enables the water level of the chamber to recede until it is level with the lower waters. The downriver gates then open and the boat departs.

Sometimes, conventional locks are built in a series of 2 or 3 and are referred to as flight locks. They can raise or lower boats in stages over a greater height. An example of this can be seen at Healey Falls.

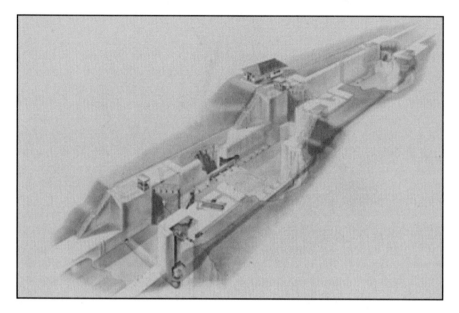

Hydraulic Lift Locks

When there is a great difference in elevation at a given location, hydraulic lift locks are employed. Two such locations are Peterborough and Kirkfield, where the levels of the waters differ 65 feet/20 m and 49 feet/15 m respectively.

The lift lock is comprised of 2 moveable chambers side by side, which counter each other's movement.Their action is likened to weigh scales. Each chamber is approximately 140 feet/42.5m by 30 feet/9 m and carries an 8 foot/2.5 m level of water. The weight of the chamber and water totals 1,700 tons. Each chamber is supported by a massive cast iron cylinder called a ram and these are connected underground in an enclosed hydraulic system.

Boats travelling upstream enter the awaiting chamber. The entrance gate swings up into position and is sealed. The enclosed chamber on the upper level has an extra foot of water in it. An extra foot of water may not seem like very much, until you realize that it weighs 144 tons.

The upper chamber will overbalance the lower when the cross-over valve connecting the 2 rams underground is opened; the heavier upper chamber descends and the lower chamber is forced upwards.

The action of one chamber forces an equal and opposite movement of the other.

The ascending chamber stops one foot short of the top and when the upper gates are open, an extra foot of water will flow in to bring the level of water in the chamber to that of the upper reach. Boats exit the chamber and craft headed downstream take their place for the descent to the lower reach.

The descending chamber will stop one foot above the level of the lower reach. When the chamber gates are swung open, the extra foot of water flows out, bringing the water level in the chamber to that of the lower reach.

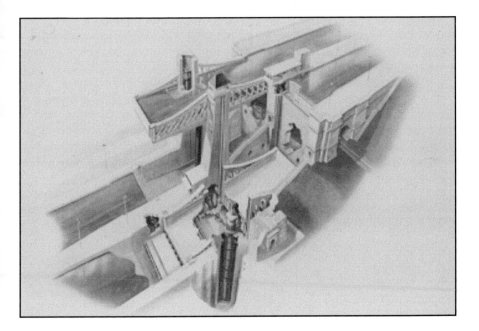

Lockmasters

● ● ● ● ● ● ● ● ● ● ● ● ● ● ● ● ● ● ●

Probably one of the most important elements of the Trent-Severn Waterway, apart from the water, is the network of lockmasters. The people who oversee and operate the locks are responsible for keeping everything running smoothly. That is no easy task, especially at popular locks during peak tourist season, foresight, extreme organization, lots of patience and a sense of humour are necessary.

Most of the lock staff are native to the area they serve and know the waters very well. During the summer, they work up to 12 hours a day. They can answer just about any question about the waterway a boater might pose.

The lovely parklands, campsites, and picnic areas are maintained by the lockmasters and their staff. They are proud of the grounds around their lockstations and their personal interest shows in the well-kept lawns and gardens.

Many people come by car to watch lock operations and this means the lockmasters must work to an audience. Enforcing rules can be difficult under any circumstances, but doing so before an audience can be gruelling, at times.

Lockmasters and their staff are most helpful and work together to ensure our comfort and safety. All locks are connected by phone, so they can alert each other of approaching boats.

Your co-operation at the locks contributes to a speedier and safer lock-through for everyone.

The CANADIAN CANOE MUSEUM
Le MUSÉE CANADIEN *du* CANOT

A MUSEUM IN THE MAKING

The Canadian Canoe Museum is a "Museum In The Making", featuring a selection of canoies and kayaks representing segments of our Canadian heritage. The museum houses the largest collection of canoes and kayaks in the world. As the Museum develops, preliminary exhibits have been established for visitors to enjoy. Come and experience " In the Time of the Kayak", the Great Fur Trade, the evolution of the modern canoe in Peterborough, and more.

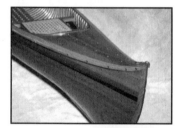

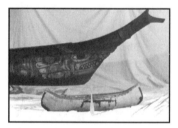

OPEN - 10:00 a.m. to 5:00 p.m., daily , July & August
Admission - donation to help out development fund.

910 Monaghan Rd., Box 1664,
Peterborough, ON, K9J 7S4

For Information Call 705-748-9153

Canoe Country

●●●●●●●●●●●●●●●●●

Canoeing is enjoying renewed popularity everywhere. People from all walks of life and ages are getting into the sport for the first time or rediscovering canoes are still as much fun as when they learned to paddle years ago at summer camp. The sheltered Trent-Severn Waterway offers canoeists a great paddle and exploration opportunity. The waterway can be explored in sections on day or weekend trips or plan the entire 240 mile/386 km trip for an extended paddle experience of a lifetime.

The convenient location of communities along the waterway corridor offers less ambitious travellers the chance to go a bit upscale and stay in quality bed and breakfast establishments or country inns located along the system. Provisions are also readily available so no real need for heavy supply packs. For those interested in camping while retracing the route of explorers like Samuel de Champlain who covered much of the waterway in the 1600s, lock stations and provincial campgrounds along the way are great places to overnight safely and in relative comfort. Lock stations have well kept grassy areas where tents can be pitched plus there are washroom facilities, fresh water and picnic tables. Some locks even have canoe rollers installed to ease a portage if not locking through.

In Lakefield and Peterborough there are municipal campgrounds and good beaches to welcome canoe travellers as well as Serpent Mounds Provincial Park on Rice Lake, the Indian River and Ferris Park at Campbellford, just to name a few. This section of the waterway offers paddlers a really good long weekend excursion opportunity. The Trent-Severn's diverse heritage, various land formations and variety of ecosystems makes this region of Central Ontario an ideal choice for a heritage canoeing experience. (cont')

Paddle with a friend

For those wanting to chart a course by canoe but without a canoe, a quick call to the tourist information centres listed at the back of this guide will result in directions to the many "outfitters" who can supply appropriate canoes and equipment. Some even offer guide services and can make arrangements for pick ups and drop offs enabling canoeists to spend more time on the water soaking up all the waterway has to offer those interested in this slower mode of transportation.

According to recent surveys appearing in *Boating Industry Magazine* canoeing now ranks 33rd out of the top 54 participation sports in North America with close to eight million people actively involved in this recreational activity. It is a growing sport with spending on equipment averaging more more than $8 million annually. Not bad for an industry that got its start right here on the Trent-Severn Waterway.

Peterborough is considered to be the birthplace of the modern canoe and for years was the home of the world famous Peterborough Canoe Company where fine hand crafted cedar strip canoes of all types were distributed worldwide. The advent of fiberglass construction and

mass production resulted in the plant's closure in the 1960s ending this glorious era of Canadian canoe building. For those willing to scout the region they will still find these types of wooden canoes being built as the tradition continues on a smaller scale by dedicated craftsmen.

paddle in solitude   The Canadian Canoe Museum also calls the Trent-Severn home and is being developed in Peterborough in the old Outboard Marine Corporation factory. This centre, in the heart of the city, houses a collection of canoes from just about everywhere and is considered the finest collection in the world under one roof. When completed the Canadian Canoe Museum will be a $7 million centre with an indoor river and canoe skills training pond along with heritage canoe displays and settings.

For arm chair canoeists still contemplating the sport or those already converted, the Friends of the Trent-Severn Waterway is a good source of canoeing information. Well known Canadian canoeist and naturalist, Kevin Callan resides in Peterborough and has written a number of canoe tripping books well worth reading. They are available through the FTSW's 1-800-663-2628 free access line, at its Nautical Nooks along the waterway and at your favourite book store. *Cottage Country Canoe Routes* gives an in depth look at canoe routes in the Georgian Bay, Muskoka, Haliburton and Kawartha regions. *Up The Creek—A Paddler's Guide to Ontario* guides white water fanatics down rushing rivers, seasoned trippers across remote lakes and family canoeists on perfect weekend outings. A good companion book published by FTSW—-The Trent-Severn Waterway: *An Environmental Exploration*, explores the geology, plants, animals, their habitats, human impacts and water quality of the waterway. The book also features five fascinating ecotours designed for canoeists, boaters, hikers, bikers and car travellers.

The Victoria County department of tourism has published a "canoe routes" guide to the Burnt and Gull Rivers that flow into the Trent-Severn. It outlines a series of day and weekend adventure trips, distances covered, portages and travel times. For this informative package contact Victoria County Tourism, 26 Francis Street, Box 9000, Lindsay, Ontario, K8V 5R8 or call (705) 324-9411, extension 233. The canoe is celebrated each year at a number of canoe festivals on the waterway. The most popular is the Heritage Canoe Festival usually held the second weekend of May at the Peterborough Lift Lock Visitor Centre. The festival offers 3 days of films, indoor displays and on water demonstrations and guest speakers covering all facets of canoeing. There's always something of interest for the experienced or novice canoe enthusiast.

a deserved rest at sunset

WINTER FUN ON THE TRENT-SEVERN

Though you can't cruise the Trent-Severn by boat in the winter there are a lot of fun things you can do. The list includes winter hiking, cross-country skiing, snowmobiling, ice fishing and of course an abundance of winter festivals and carnivals. Ontario's longest running winter carnival takes place in February in Penetanguishene.

As the waterway provides a link from Georgian Bay to Lake Ontario, intricate snowmobile trails do as well. Over 30 local snowmobile clubs share resources to make up this vast system of trails. Information on snowmobiling in Ontario can be found by contacting the Ontario Federation of Snowmobile Clubs, Box 94, Barrie, Ontario, L4M 4S9.

Ice Fishing is also a big attraction to the system. Lake Simcoe is know as 'Canada's Ice Fishing Capital' Trout, whitefish, perch, walley, and pike, are among the fish to be caught beneath the icy surface. Huts are easily available and some great local derbies take place, many centred in the Town of Georgina, on Lake Simcoe. Lake Scugog is also an Ice Fishing locale.

There are some great cross-country skiing trails at conservation areas all along the waterway. Trail maps and information are available from the local conservation authorities.

The Trent-Severn Waterway is an awesome destination in the summer, if you enjoy it then take advantage of some winter activities, local hospitality and the beauty of the system under a blanket of snow.

Try some winter 'Land Cruising' to check-out and pre-plan your summer vacation destination.

Area

3

Peterborough to Buckhorn

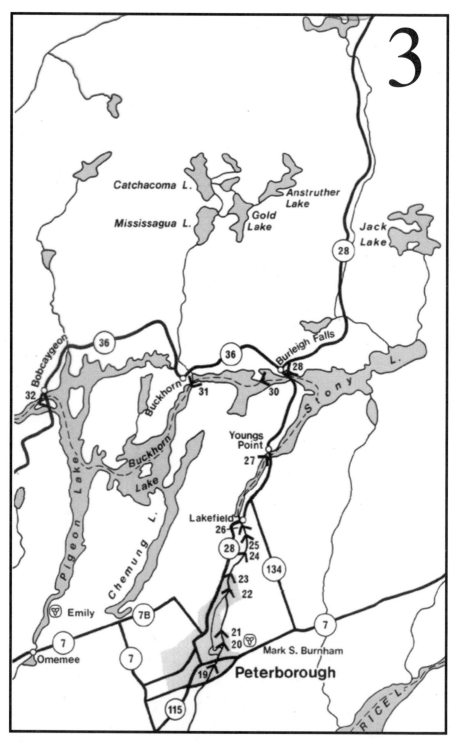

3

Catchacoma L.

Anstruther
Lake

Mississagua L.

Gold
Lake

Jack
Lake

28

36

36

Burleigh Falls

Bobcaygeon

32

Buckhorn

31

30

28

Stony L.

Buckhorn
Lake

Youngs
Point

27

Pigeon Lake

Chemung L.

Lakefield

26

28

25
24

134

23

22

Emily

7B

21

20

Mark S. Burnham

7

Omemee

7

7

19

Peterborough

115

RICE L.

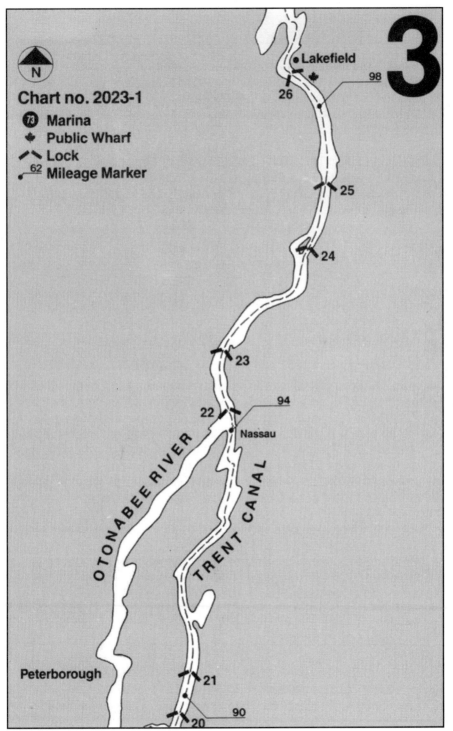

Chart no. 2023-1

74 Marina
🍁 Public Wharf
Lock
•62 Mileage Marker

Lakefield
98
26
25
24
23
22
94
Nassau
OTONABEE RIVER
TRENT CANAL
Peterborough
21
90
20

Nassau Mills: Lock #22

'Beautiful Nassau', as it has been nicknamed by boaters, has 7.5 acres of excellent parkland complete picnic tables. It has one of the longest approach walls on the waterway and can accommodate many boats. This is a manual lock and the staff members are often asked if circling the sweeps makes them dizzy. Their standard reply is that it is a good way to unwind.

From the lock, it is a short quarter mile/half km walk to Trent University where there is public transportation into Peterborough. Trent University's Wildlife Sanctuary can also be visited, keep your eyes open for horned owls, cooper hawks and other species.

Otonabee: Lock #23

Tie-up facilities at this secluded lock are limited but, there is a small bay a few hundred yards upstream which is ideal for anchoring.

Douro: Lock #24

The lock-through time here is approximately 12 minutes and the water levels differ by 12 feet/3.6 m. Most boaters tie up in the upstream reach because it is closer to washrooms. There are good camp facilities for boaters who are interested in overnight camping. The tie-up area downstream is more secluded if you prefer privacy to convenience. Centennial Marsh is located at the lock. It is a great spot to view marsh wild life and for frog watching or listening. The winding drive past locks 22-24 on River Road/Nassau Mills Road is beautiful and scenic, great for a long walk or bike ride.

Sawyer Creek: Lock #25

Prevailing west winds make this lock a fairly gusty one. There is usually a heavy cross current on the downstream side of the lock in the spring. Lock-through time is about 20 minutes.

Lakefield: Lock #26

Although located in the village, this is a very secluded lock station. Just upstream on the eastbank is the Village of Lakefield marina located in the heart of the town where all amenities are easily accessible.

Lakefield

●●●●●●●●●●●●●●●●●●●

An eclectic blend of the modern and the traditional, the Village of Lakefield is nestled along the banks of the peaceful Otonabee River. Boaters can moor at the village's new marina and explore the entire village on foot.

A light stroll along the riverbank reveals a number of restful locations including a deck beside a comprehensive visitor information centre,operated by the Lakefield and District Chamber of Commerce. There you'll find information on accommodation, dining, attractions and shopping opportunities in the village and beyond.

Lakefield's Queen Street is the centre of activity in this bustling community. Artists, artisans and merchants provide hours of enjoyable browsing. From Chinese food to fish and chips to traditional cooking, Lakefield's selection of restaurants is sure to satisfy any craving you may have. Whether it's hardware or eyewear, the village is large enough to offer important products and services you may need along your way. Groceries, postal services, laundry, spirits, banking, and church services are always handy. The unparalleled level of personal service will keep you coming back to Lakefield again and again.

Lakefield & District

Visit us year-round!

Visitor Information

Call **(705) 652-6963**
or write to:
Box 537 Lakefield, ON K0L 2H0
Located at Hwy. #28 (Bridge St.) & the river

Lakefield Park, offering camping and picnic sites, has a good sandy beach and is located across from the marina. There is a flea market at the fair grounds every Sunday.

Lakefield also maintains some historically significant sites. The most obvious of these is Christ Church, situated on Queen Street, right downtown. Built under the direction of patriarch Major Samuel Strickland, this stone building quickly became the focus of the community. With seating for about 100, the first service was held on Christmas Eve 1854. The church, now lovingly maintained by volunteers from the district, serves as a museum showcasing a number of historical artifacts including the writing desk of Catherine Parr Traill. It is open to the public daily from Victoria Day weekend to Labour Day, from 1 pm to 4 pm.

Christ Church, Lakefield

Lakefield has been the home of other famous Canadian writers such as Susanna Moodie and Margaret Laurence. Partake in the 'Remembering Margaret' Festival taking place in July.

Naturalists will appreciate the current efforts to preserve a provincially significant wetland that is situated near the Lakefield Park and Campground. Plans for a viewing tower, hiking pathways, a canoe launch and a butterfly garden are underway.

You can find Lakefield on Hwys 28 and 507 and just west of Hwy 134.

The Village of Lakefield Marina is the best place to dock to be close to all the community has to offer. At the same time the marina is in a peaceful park like setting. With an information centre on site, you will be well informed as to what is going on in Lakefield.

Lakefield Marina welcomes houseboats and offers pumpout service. Though gas is not available here it can be found right next door at Toth Marine.

S teamboats, from the arrival of the first settlers in the area, were a part of the scenery playing host to city dwellers and farmers alike, all seeking adventure. Today, you are able to cruise Stoney Lake, and from Lakefield to Young's Point in the luxury and style that have been popular for generations. Fenelon Falls, Bobcaygeon Boat Cruises are also available, as are Scugog River boat cruises aboard the Skylark VIII. Don't miss the 'Cruising' feature at the beginning of this guide.

Steamboat at Young's Point

Stoney Lakes Navigation Company's Admiral Sir John

Young's Point
● ● ● ● ● ● ● ● ● ● ● ● ● ● ● ● ●

Francis Young and his children were among the immigrants who arrived with Peter Robinson to settle in Peterborough or Scott's Mills as it was called. They arrived in 1825 and, having brought their own tools, they forged on past the settlement and settled at the rapids between Lake Katchewanooka and Clear Lake. After damming the rapids, the Youngs built a gristmill and sawmill.

The settlement grew and by the time the lumber boom was at its peak Young's Point had 3 hotels. Francis' son Patrick donated lands to the Ontario government for the construction of a lock. The original was completed in the early 1870s. Patrick Young also began an operation of steamboats for cargo and passenger service to Stoney Lake. The popularity of this area for tourists grew with the advent of steamships.

Today Young's Point is still a very popular stop with boaters and motorists. Patrick Young's house is still standing adjacent to the lock and has been transformed into a unique country shopping attraction called Lockside Trading Company. The village has a general store and post office, snack bar, restaurants, marinas and accommodation. The park grounds bordering the lock are ample and provide a scenic spot for a picnic. The old steel bridge dating back to the 1870s spans the waterway here. Now that Hwy 28 actually bypasses Young's Point, the bridge is a pedestrian connection to both sides of this historic enclave. This bridge will lead you to the Old Bridge Inn Hotel for a meal after you've finished browsing at Lockside Trading Co., a must-see for boaters and motorists. By car you can find Young's Point on Hwy 28 between Lakefield and Burleigh Falls.

Young's Point: Lock #27

Young's Point usually catches a strong north-west wind when one is blowing, so don't let it catch you off guard. Since this is a popular lock, you are advised to arrive early if you plan to stay overnight. There is a spacious park with picnic tables and barbecues at the lock and excellent restaurants and accommodation nearby. Fishing is reported to be excellent, too. Pickerel/Walleye, bass and muskie can be found in abundance around the dam and a popular pickerel haunt is at Graveyard Point, about 200 yards downstream from the bridge.

Lockside Trading Co., Young's Point

NEW OWNERS-OLD BRIDGE INN

The Old Bridge Inn Hotel is a quaint little hideaway. Originally built in 1887 by Jas. Kearney on property purchased from Robert Young. At that time it was operated as a general store known as Kearney Store. This is a wonderful, old building resonant with history.

Its new owners, Angelika and Richard Kerr, are working to capture that authentic charm of a by-gone era, without sacrificing any modern day comforts. This inn is a 7 room Bed & Breakfast with a fully licensed dining room open for lunch and dinner. Dining is casual but of high quality and service.

The Kerr's goal is to offer the community a place where guests can enjoy an excellent meal after a long day of work, boating or cottaging as well as a unique spot for those special occasion dinners and lunches. Small banquets, and corporate meeting facilities are offered as well. This Inn, with its beautiful setting on the banks of the Trent-Severn Waterway, is an ideal spot for wedding receptions. Bed & Breakfast patrons are treated to continental breakfast with their overnight accommodation.

The Old Bridge Inn Hotel is an ideal home base while exploring the lakelands or visiting or partaking in the many local attractions or events in the Peterborough and the Kawartha Lakes region.

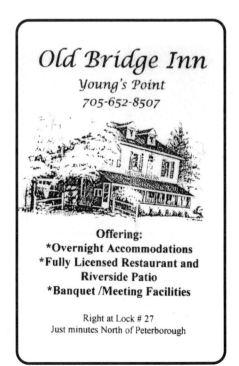

Old Bridge Inn
Young's Point
705-652-8507

Offering:
*Overnight Accommodations
*Fully Licensed Restaurant and Riverside Patio
*Banquet /Meeting Facilities

Right at Lock # 27
Just minutes North of Peterborough

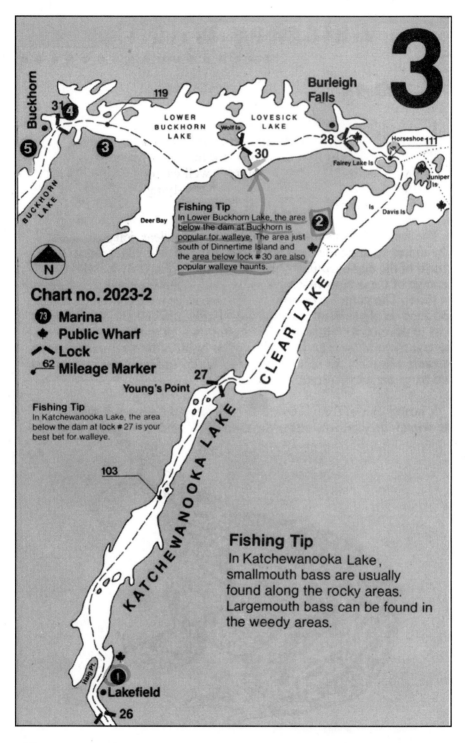

3

Buckhorn

Burleigh Falls

119

31 ④

③

⑤

LOWER BUCKHORN LAKE

LOVESICK LAKE

Wolf Is

30

28

Horseshoe 111

Fairey Lake Is

Juniper Is

Is

Davis Is

BUCKHORN LAKE

Deer Bay

Fishing Tip
In Lower Buckhorn Lake, the area below the dam at Buckhorn is popular for walleye. The area just south of Dinnertime Island and the area below lock #30 are also popular walleye haunts.

N

Chart no. 2023-2

⑦³ **Marina**

✦ **Public Wharf**

⌒ **Lock**

⌒⁶² **Mileage Marker**

Fishing Tip
In Katchewanooka Lake, the area below the dam at lock #27 is your best bet for walleye.

27

Young's Point

C L E A R   L A K E

103

K A T C H E W A N O O K A   L A K E

Fishing Tip

In Katchewanooka Lake, smallmouth bass are usually found along the rocky areas. Largemouth bass can be found in the weedy areas.

Hazg Pt.

① ●**Lakefield**

26

Chart no. 2023-2

MARINA	☾	H	⚡	⛽	⛽	⚓	🚰	⛵	🏗	🔧	🚻	🛏	🍴	🛒
❶ Lakefield Marina 705-620-0330	✓	✓	✓			✓	✓	✓		✓	✓	✓	✓	✓
❷ Kawartha Park Marina 705-654-3549	✓	✓	✓	✓			✓	✓		✓	✓	✓		✓
❸ Reach Harbour 705-657-8747	✓	✓	✓	✓	✓	✓	✓	✓	✓	✓	✓	✓		✓
❹ Sunrise Resort 705-657-8713	✓		✓	✓		✓	✓			✓	✓			✓
❺ Buckhorn Yacht Harbour 705-657-8752	✓		✓	✓		✓	✓	✓	✓	✓	✓	✓	✳	✳

Burleigh Falls

●●●●●●●●●●●●●●●●●●

L ock 28, at the lovely hamlet of Burleigh Falls, will lift you 24 feet/7 m from Stoney Lake to Lovesick Lake. Burleigh Falls may be small in stature, but it's big in spirit. Every August, hundreds of spectators come to catch the excitement of the Annual Whitewater Kayak races on the rapids. The bass fishing on Lovesick Lake at Burleigh Falls is excellent.

There are motels, restaurants, groceries and campsites within walking distance of the public wharf.

For details on **Stoney Lake** and area refer to Chart 2023-3 and the pages following. This is a big lake and well worth exploring; a centre for historic resorts, boat cruises, fine dining, cottaging, and water sports of all types.

Picture Perfect Day on Lovesick Lake

Petroglyphs Provincial Park
●●●●●●●●●●●●●●●●●●

Petroglyphs, or 'carvings in rock', are the attracting feature of this park. Petroglyphs Park has the largest concentration of Indian rock carvings in Canada. Originally carved or chipped into soft, crystalline limestone, the figures and symbols remain a fascinating puzzle to this day. The carvings were done about 500 to 1000 years ago and the symbols are thought to represent some cultural aspect of the carvers. The Algonkian Indians, comprised of many tribes, were semi-nomadic. They followed game and travelled to seasonal hunting grounds. Many symbols are believed to represent good and evil spirits which figured prominently in their daily lives.

Since no one knows for sure, you could give free reign to your imagination and come up with your own theory regarding these enigmatic symbols. Some suspect that the symbols are actually an ancient form of map, depicting river routes, hunting grounds, food sources and burial grounds. Whatever your speculation, it is certainly worth some entertaining reflection.

Petroglyphs Provincial Park

Established for day-use only, the park has no campsites, it is open from early May through mid October. Though there is no camping at Petroglyphs Provincial Park, there are picnic facilities and hiking trails. Parks staff are available to assist in interpretation and special evening programs take place to identify the numerous carvings not visible during the day. Petroglyphs Provincial Park is off Highway 28 north of Burleigh Falls on Northey's Bay Road. Call (705) 877-2552 for information.

Burleigh Falls: Lock #28

In the past, there were two locks here; when the locks were mechanized the two became one. That is why you will not find lock 29 today.

The drop from the upper reach to the lower reach at the lock is 24 feet/7 metres. While the lock is being emptied, there is a fairly strong current in the lower reach. There is very little turbulence in the lock chamber however, due to the double floor construction.

During peak summer periods, it is best to tie up early to ensure docking. The Petroglyphs are about 15 miles/24 kms from this lock.

Lovesick: Lock #30

Lovesick Lock remains one of the prettiest and most isolated of all the stations on the Waterway. The staff who operate the smallest lift (3.5 ft./1 m) travel back and forth by boat from the Burleigh Falls Lock.

The lock itself is situated right on an island and is a very popular tie-up spot, with natural unmarked trails on Wolf Island providing an opportunity to stretch and stroll. There are 5 dams here with names such as Sunrise, Sunset, Black Duck and Grey Duck, as well as a small canoe chute complete with rollers to assist fishermen in their quest for the elusive muskellunge. Boaters should approach the lock at a dead slow speed to eliminate wake damage and, during high water flows, be aware of the strong downstream current.

muskie

Buckhorn: Lock #31

You will have to arrive very early to ensure tie-up at this lock. It is one of the busiest on the waterway and most popular. The tie-up on both sides of the lock are close to grocery stores, liquor store, hardware store and restaurants.

There is usually a stiff breeze blowing, particularly on the upstream side of the lock. Houseboats should enter the lock chamber on the side to which the wind is blowing, since they will eventually be blown to that side anyway. Pay particular attention to all directions given by the lockmaster. It will make passage a lot easier for everyone concerned.

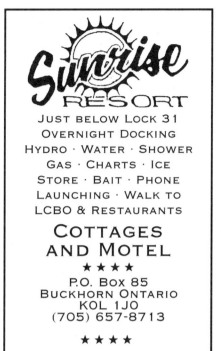

Buckhorn, Lock 31.

Buckhorn

●●●●●●●●●●●●●●●●●●●

The village of Buckhorn is situated between Lower Buckhorn Lake and Buckhorn Lake at the junction of Hwys 36 and 507.. It was once called Hall's Falls after John Hall, who settled in the area in 1830 and established a sawmill and gristmill. As the story goes, John was a keen hunter and began to mount the antlers of his finest bucks on the wall of his mill. Before long, passersby were referring to the area as Buckhorn Falls.

This village is a busy place in the summer due to the over-whelming popularity of the Buckhorn Wildlife Art Festival and Sale, so you'll find plenty of accommodation, restaurants and service facilities in the vicinity.

The Gallery-on-the-Lake, just 1.8 miles/3 kms east of Buckhorn, welcomes you into their gallery to view paintings by many renowned Canadian artists, such as Michael Dumas, Edwin Matthews, Jake Vanderbrink, Silvia Armeni, Mary Lampman and Mary Kendrick. There is a dock for visiting boaters.

Edwin and Barbara Matthews were the initiators of the first Buckhorn Wildlife Art Festival and Sale. They were approached about an art show to raise funds for the Buckhorn Community Centre mortgage. The event was so successful that it has become an annual festival attracting visitors from all over Canada, the U.S. and Europe. Over 100 professional artists demonstrate and show wildlife, contemporary landscape and native paintings, as well as carvings and pottery. The festival is held annually the 2nd weekend after the Civic holiday weekend in August at the Buckhorn Community Centre. Which is just 5 minutes from the waterway. Bus service from the lock to the Festival is available. There are creative activities for young children, a refreshment marquee, and the facility is wheelchair accessible.

Buckhorn is home to a variety of eating places and stores to meet your needs. Groceries, hardware, liquor/beer outlet, drug store and post office are all within walking distance of lock 31. The community centre runs a weekly bingo on Wednesday evenings. During July and August, Thursday evening is movie night at the Centre. We know you will enjoy your stay in Beautiful Buckhorn. Don't forget to have your picture taken by the "Buck".

Buckhorn "Buck" beside Cody Inn

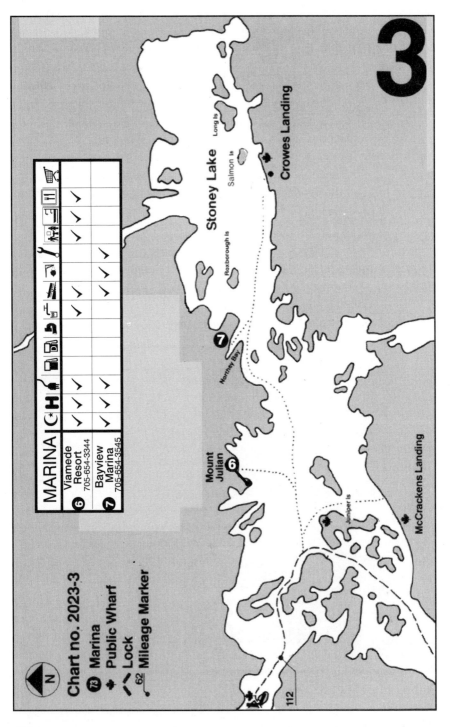

3

N

Chart no. 2023-3

🏪 Marina
⚓ Public Wharf
Lock
62 Mileage Marker

MARINA	🛈	⛽	🏪	🛠			🔧	🏕	🍴	🛒
6 Viamede Resort 705-654-3344	✓	✓		✓				✓	✓	
7 Bayview Marina 705-654-3545	✓	✓		✓	✓		✓	✓	✓	

Stoney Lake

Long Is

Salmon Is

Crowes Landing

Roxborough Is

Northey Bay

7

Mount Julian

6

McCrackens Landing

Juniper Is

112

Crowes Landing
• •

This scenic little community, nestled on the south shore of Stoney Lake, has a public wharf at the landing. Crowes Landing has marinas, a store, good accommodation and restaurants, as well as churches and a golf course not far from the public wharf. On this picturesque lake there are some outstanding country resorts such as Irwin Inn seen below. The north shore at Mount Julian is host to Viamede Resort another breathtaking country resort.

Navigation Note:
Stoney Lake is known to have large granite rocks lying just below the surface of the water. When leaving the main channel proceed with caution.

Irwin Inn, aeriael view

Visit Viamede Resort
during your boating vacation

Nestled on the tree-lined north shore of Stoney Lake,
Viamede Resort and Conference Centre dates back to 1860,
and is considered the Crown Jewel of the Kawarthas. It is also
one of the very few original resorts remaining that served
travellers from the many steamboats of the past who
regularly threaded their way among the 1100
islands dotting Stoney Lake. Viamede
still is a popular stopping place for
vacationing boaters with
its ample docking facilities.
has become a favourite
destination of boaters
travelling through the
Trent/Severn Waterway.
Reasonable overnight
dockage and
accommodation rates
presents boating guests an
opportunity to enjoy a
wide range of Viamede's
recreational facilities. Any
stop-over wouldn't be complete
without sampling a delicious
meal in their dining room. A pleasant finale to your visit
could also include joining in the fun at the Boathouse Bar
And Galley at the water's edge or enjoying a relaxing evening
on the elevated patio.

If time permits Viamede provides an excellent base from
which to visit the many area attractions. Interesting day trips
could include a visit to the 1,000 year old rock carvings in the
Petroglyph Provincial Park, the Gallery on the Lake or
shopping in local boutiques such as the Cedarwood Gift Shop
or The Lockside Trading Co.

Within the resort boundaries, visitors have a wide area of
activities available which include hiking, mountain biking,
horseback riding, tennis, badminton, volleyball or enjoying a
50 foot sports pool. So, if you are looking for a relaxing break
in your boating vacation, remember to include Viamede in
your travel plans.

TRENT SEVERN WATERWAY

If you're planning a day trip, a weekend or just a stop over while travelling through the Trent System then consider Viamede Resort.

We are located between the Young's Point Lock, No. 27 and Burleigh Falls Lock, No. 28 on the north shore of Stoney Lake.

DIRECTIONS TO OUR DOCK: On map 2023, Sheet 3 of 3, Stoney Lake: locate marker C200 turn and go due east. At that point go to marker CJ1 then turn due north to Mount Julian.

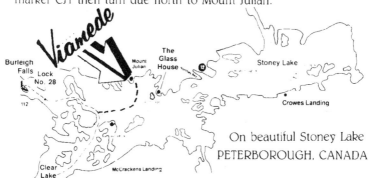

On beautiful Stoney Lake
PETERBOROUGH, CANADA

Facilities:

- ~ Overnight Dock space for up to 30 boats (8ft. draft)
- ~ Shore Power (15-30 AMP)
- ~ Washrooms, Showers, Ice, Water
- ~ Boaters Galley with TV and Lounge Area
- ~ Designated BBQ Area
- ~ Kids Recreation Program Avail. in July/Aug for a nominal charge
- ~ Complimentary use of canoes and paddle boats
- ~ Riding Stable Open Daily in July and August
- ~ 50' Sports Pool/Hot Tub/Sauna
- ~ Full range of rooms for overnight stays
- ~ Wet Jet Rentals
- ~ Fully Licenced Dining Room
- ~ Boathouse Bar & Galley with full food service - Open Daily
- ~ Tuck Shoppe
- ~ Special Off-Season Rates

SPECIAL EVENTS

Spring Launch

Kick-off the season with a Boaters. Sports Day followed by a large outdoor B-B-Que.

Captains Table

Join us for our annual Wind-up to the season with a Delicious meal served at the Captains Table plus complimentary wine & cheese reception.

Viamede Resort

For Dockage or Diningroom Reservations Call

(705) 652-1166

C.B. Channel 10
VHF Channel 68

ONTARIO

BOATING FORUM

A VOICE FOR RECREATIONAL BOATERS IN ONTARIO

The Ontario Boating Forum is the only organization in the province whose sole purpose is to safeguard the rights of all recreational boaters.

With a wide variety of issues impacting boating today --safety, licencing, pollution control, government cutbacks, rising user fees and taxes--the Ontario Boating Forum is there in a proactive way to make sure the voice of recreational boaters is heard!

OBF's success is dependent upon an aggressive concerned membership.

Are you concerned about the future of recreational boating? Protect your recreation and boating rights. Call or write for a brochure and membership application. A modest $20.00 membership includes quarterly newsletters and is a worthwhile investment in helping protect the future of boating in Ontario.

ONTARIO BOATING FORUM

P.O. Box 111, Station A
Etobicoke, Ontario
M9C 4V2

Phone: (905) 820-3192
Fax: (905) 820-4817

Area

4

Buckhorn
to
Bobcaygeon

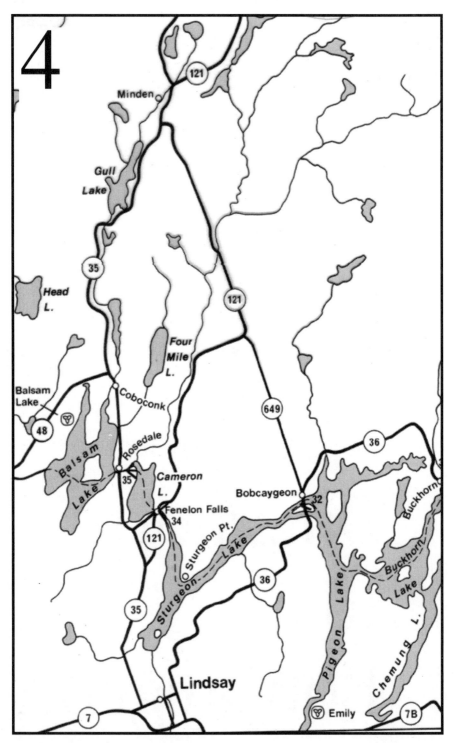

4

Minden

121

Gull
Lake

35

Head
L.

Four
Mile
L.

Balsam
Lake

48

Coboconk

Rosedale

Balsam

Lake

35

Cameron
L.

Fenelon Falls

34

121

Sturgeon Pt.

Sturgeon

Lake

Bobcaygeon

32

36

36

121

649

Buckhorn

Buckhorn
Lake

Pigeon

Lake

Chemung L.

35

Lindsay

7

Emily

7B

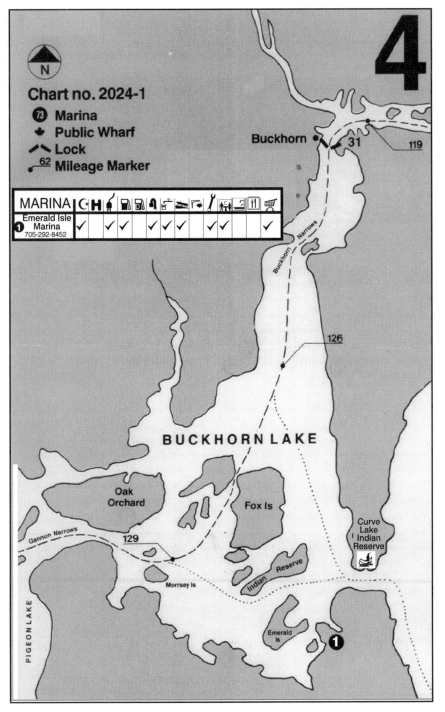

4

N

Chart no. 2024-1

- 🅰 Marina
- ⚓ Public Wharf
- Lock
- 62 Mileage Marker

MARINA	G	H													
① Emerald Isle Marina 705-292-8452	✓		✓	✓		✓	✓	✓		✓	✓				✓

Buckhorn ● 31 119

Buckhorn Narrows

126

BUCKHORN LAKE

Oak Orchard

Fox Is

Curve Lake Indian Reserve

Gannon Narrows 129

Morrsey Is

Indian Reserve

PIGEON LAKE

Emerald Is ①

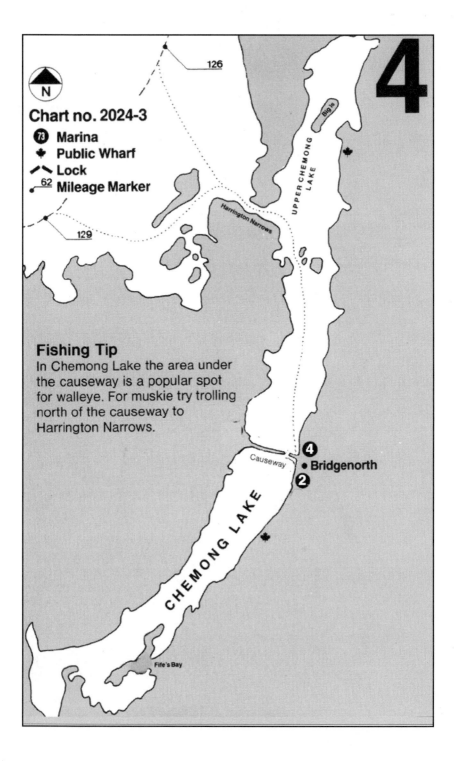

4

N

Chart no. 2024-3

73 Marina
✣ Public Wharf
⌒ Lock
_62_ Mileage Marker

126

129

Big Is

UPPER CHEMONG LAKE

Harrington Narrows

Fishing Tip
In Chemong Lake the area under
the causeway is a popular spot
for walleye. For muskie try trolling
north of the causeway to
Harrington Narrows.

Causeway

4
● **Bridgenorth**
2

CHEMONG LAKE

Fife's Bay

Chart no. 2024-3

MARINA	C	H	⛽	🛢	⚓	🚿	🛥	🪝	🔧	🚻	🛏	🍴	🛒
❷ Old Causeway Marina 705-292-5390	✓	✓	✓	✓		✓	✓		✓	✓	✓	✓	
❹ Dutch Marine 705-292-7111	✓		✓	✓		✓	✓	✓	✓	✓	✓	✓	

Once clearing Buckhorn lock 31 boaters are entering another expanse of lakes, including Buckhorn, Chemong and Pigeon, that provide waterway explorers the opportunity to spend a day or two experiencing all this area of the Kawartha chain of lakes has to offer.

Following the main channel boaters have a number of options. On the eastern shore is Curve Lake Indian Reserve, a site well worth visiting. From there through Harrington Narrows , boaters will head in a southerly direction down Chemong Lake to the village of Bridgenorth and its variety of offerings.

Secluded Cove

Curve Lake Indian Reserve

• • • • • • • • • • • • • • • • •

Just south of Buckhorn, at the junction of Buckhorn and Chemong Lakes, you'll find the Whetung Art Gallery & Ojibwa Craft Centre on the Curve Lake Indian Reserve. Keep an eye out for the large public dock. It is just a short walk from the Whetung Art Gallery and from other local shops.

Whetung's is an experience not to be missed. The Centre, made of local stone and logs, is guarded by 30-foot totem poles which flank the entrance. Inside, you'll find finely crafted souvenir articles from across the continent. There are hand-sewn moccasins, fur and leather clad dolls, Eskimo carvings, the complete Hudson Bay line, Quebec wooden carvings, Canadian crystal, pottery and finely crafted jewellery. Also available are paintings by native artists, limited edition prints and stone carvings by Joseph Jacobs.

Whetung Art Gallery & Ojibwa Crafts

The Museum section of the Centre contains many wonderful examples of native handiwork and art of bygone years. To round off your trip to the Whetung Centre, you can enjoy a delicious Indian Corn soup and Indian fried bread in the Tea Room. The centre is open all year, 7 days a week.

This First Nations Community is but one of several along the waterway. Others include Alderville First Nation on the south shore of Rice Lake, and the Hiawatha First Nation on the north shore of Rice lake. This band also operates the Serpent Mounds Provincial Park. Rama near Orillia, and Scugog Island are also home to First Nations communities as well as Georgina Island on Lake Simcoe.

Bridgenorth

●●●●●●●●●●●●●●●●●●

Bridgenorth is a small community located on the east shore of Chemong Lake about 7 miles/11 kms south of the Curve Lake Reserve. There are churches, grocery stores, shops, a post office, medical centre, veterinarian, liquor store and beer store for your convenience. Restaurants from fast food to fine dining can be found here as well. There are a number of marinas at or near Bridgenorth. By car you can get to Bridgenorth by taking Chemong Road north from Peterborough.

Old Causeway Marine provides a good selection of rental boats for anglers driving to the area to tie into the excellent pickerel, bass and "big" muskie that can still be caught on this lake.

For an evening of great dining we can recommend Chemong Lodge Restaurant situated in a 100 year old cottage estate just steps away from Champlain Park where this famous explorer camped in the 1600s en route with a native war party destined for engagements in what is now known as northern New York State.

Old Causeway Marine, Bridgenorth

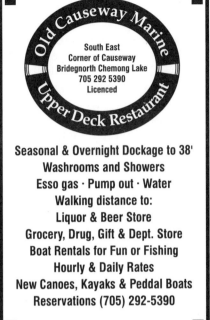
Navigation Note

Chemong Lake is about 14 miles/22 kms long and approximately 3/4 of a mile/1 km wide. There are only a few islands in the lake and it offers excellent cruising.

Oak Orchard

● ● ● ● ● ● ● ● ● ● ● ● ● ● ● ● ● ●

Retracing your route through Harrington Narrows boaters will pass marker 129 before going under the high span Gannon Narrows Bridge. Before the bridge on the north shore is the 53 acre Oak Orchard property. This historic setting is once again destined for redevelopment. Despite its appearance today this property has been the site of a variety of summer resorts dating back to the late 1800s. Fire destroyed one; another was transformed by the Outboard Marine Corporation into one of its corporate retreats and product testing centres. Fifty years ago this place was visited by many top name Hollywood stars, guests of OMC executives. If you listen closely some say you can still catch the faint whine of an outboard racer skimming across the water in front of Oak Orchard - where the world's top outboard speed record was set by OMC test "pilots".

In the mid 1980s it was again revitalized when Canada's largest charter houseboat fleet called Oak Orchard home with 144 vessels. Since the company moved on, the historic lodge was demolished as well as other on site buildings. In the back of the property a huge man-made harbour was excavated for the houseboat fleet. It is accessed by a narrow channel that is now grown over. During its dredging one of the shovel operators reported scooping up a muskie that literally hung out over both sides of his back hoe bucket. Now that's a big fish!

Oak Orchard's future is now looking bright again. Developers are planning a 100 room four season resort for this strategically located recreation property plus a casino and full service marine centre.

Architects rendering of new Oak Orchard resort

140

Once under the bridge and through Gannon Narrows you are out into Pigeon Lake. This is a large body of water running north-south with Bobcaygeon at the top end. To your left boaters will likely see groups of boats at anchor south of marker 132. That is because there is a super sandbar in the middle of the lake that is ideal for an afternoon's anchorage and swimming. It is a local meeting place for many boaters.

Back on the main route to Bobcaygeon check charts carefully as there are numerous shoals that can eat props and lower units if the captain is inattentive. Look out for Three Sisters Shoal. You will also see Big Island on the right side. This island is also sometimes called Boyd Island since the Boyd lumber family once used this island to try and raise 'Beefalo' but the experiment proved unsuccessful partly because the animals kept managing to swim away. In Bobcaygeon there remains almost nothing of the old Boyd Mansion estate that had a roof top viewing area to try and keep an eye on 'Beefalo' activities on the island.

Before entering the Little Bob Channel boaters can opt to cruise the north shore of Pigeon Lake that leads to Nogies Creek and Big and Little Bald Lakes.

Oak Orchard, Circa 1982

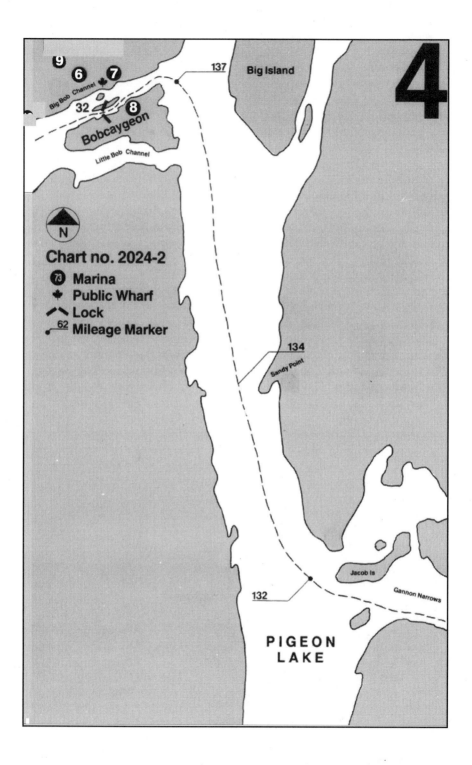

9

6 7

Big Bob Channel

137

Big Island

32

8

Bobcaygeon

Little Bob Channel

N

Chart no. 2024-2

73 Marina

Public Wharf

Lock

62 Mileage Marker

134

Sandy Point

132

Jacob Is

Gannon Narrows

PIGEON
LAKE

Chart no. 2024-2

MARINA	C★	H	🔌	⛽	⛽	⚓	🚰	🛥	📦	🔧	🚻	🛏	🍽	🛒
6 Bobcaygeon Inn 705-738-5433	✓		✓										✓	
7 Gordon Yacht Harbour 705-738-2381	✓	✓	✓	✓	✓	✓	✓	✓		✓	✓	✓	✓	✓
8 Buckeye Marine 705-738-5151								✓	✓	✓				
9 Bobcaygeon Marine 705-738-2111									✓	✓				

Bobcaygeon

• • • • • • • • • • • • • • • •

The beautiful town of Bobcaygeon lies between Pigeon Lake and Sturgeon Lake. In 1998 Bobcaygeon's lock 32 will be 165 years old, it was the first lock built on the Trent-Severn Waterway. The original wooden dam altered the conditions which gave this village its name, meaning - "shallow rapids". Comprised of 3 islands, Bobcaygeon was originally a mill town and many of its century-old homes are constructed of white pine and limestone which were lumbered and quarried locally. Some of this history can be viewed at Kawartha Settlers' Village.

Because the town has been built on 3 islands, its hospitality, naturally, avails itself to boaters. It even has a golf course which is accessible by water.

The area is an arts and crafts mecca. Watch for the signs. Bobcaygeon hosts the Ontario Open Fiddle and Step Dance Contests and the U.S./Canada Walleye Tournament. The summer calendar of events includes Bingo in several locations, bazaars and bake sales, as well as other major events such as the Home Show, a weekend of July 1st celebrations including and Arts and Crafts Show and the Ducks Unlimited Banquet and Auction, the Fall Fair and Octoberfest.

A visit to Bobcaygeon offers a wide variety of activities whether you are action-minded or just looking to unwind. Visitors can find an array of accommodations and restaurants, a liquor and beer store, laundromats, groceries, hardware, health clinic, vets, banks and many unique shops. There are 2 public beaches—Beach Park on Sturgeon Lake and Riverview Park on Little Bob River. The John Eakins Walkway at Beach Park is accessible to everyone including strollers and wheelchairs. This is a town worth exploring, there is lots to see and do.

Gordon Yacht Harbour recently underwent a significant transformation and is open to cater to the needs of seasonal as well as transient boaters. Diesel fuel is not easily found on the Trent-Severn but is available here now. The recent upgrades include expansion to the docking harbour and the opening of an all new *Harbour Doc's Seafood Restaurant*. From here it is just a short walk up the street to the refurbished Bobcaygeon Inn which offers visitors the new *Red Tomato Restaurant*, good overnight rooms and a super new spa facility and conference centre.

Bobcaygeon is located on Hwys 36 and 649 and County Roads 8 and 24.

Bobcaygeon, Lock 32

Bobcaygeon: Lock #32

The swing bridge downstream from the lock has a clearance of 11.5 feet/3.5 m . It is usually closed until someone signals 3 toots for passage through. The time involved in continually opening and closing the bridge results in long delays, so boaters going through are advised not to tarry while the bridge is open. A P.A. system is in effect here, so listen for marshalling orders from the lock staff regarding when to proceed. Boaters are asked to proceed slowly on the lower reach because this is a cottage area and wakes can be dangerous to swimming children and can also erode shorelines.

This lock is 175 feet/53 m long and invites a lot of land-based visitation. Tie-up space is good on both sides of the lock.

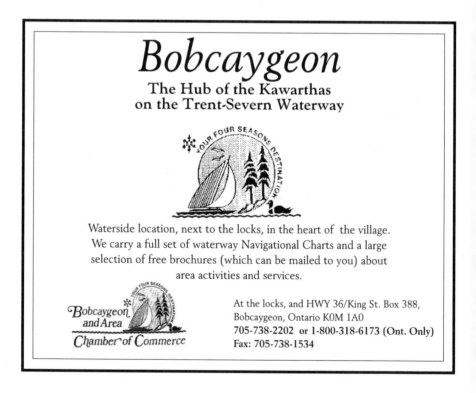

Omemee

Located at the southern end of Pigeon Lake, on the Pigeon River, Omemee has a population of about 1,000. Omemee has many shops and restaurants and more importantly, a good sense of humour. Where else could you participate in an annual worm race? This event takes place during Pioneer Days, held the weekend prior to Canada Day, when the town also hosts an outdoor dance, weather permitting, and a delicious pig roast. Call (705)799-0464 for details and schedule. Visit Omemee on Hwy 7 between Lindsay and Peterborough.

Emily Provincial Park

Just north-east of Omemee lies Emily Provincial Park. There are a number of campsites available and the majority have electricity. The park has picnic facilities, washrooms with showers, a laundromat and a playground for children. There is also a store at the park.

You will find self-guided trails at Emily which include a boardwalk over the marsh , perfect for a closer look at marsh wildlife. The park has safe swimming beaches and 2 boat launching ramps. The public wharves have shallow depths and provide docking for crafts with draughts of 2 feet or less. For further information call (705)799-5170.

Emily Park is just off Hwy 7 past Omemee on County Road 14.

Distance Chart

Approximate
(in miles)

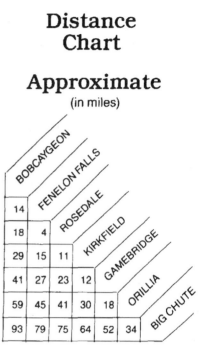

BOBCAYGEON	FENELON FALLS	ROSEDALE	KIRKFIELD	GAMEBRIDGE	ORILLIA	BIG CHUTE
14						
18	4					
29	15	11				
41	27	23	12			
59	45	41	30	18		
93	79	75	64	52	34	

Trent-Severn Houseboat Heaven

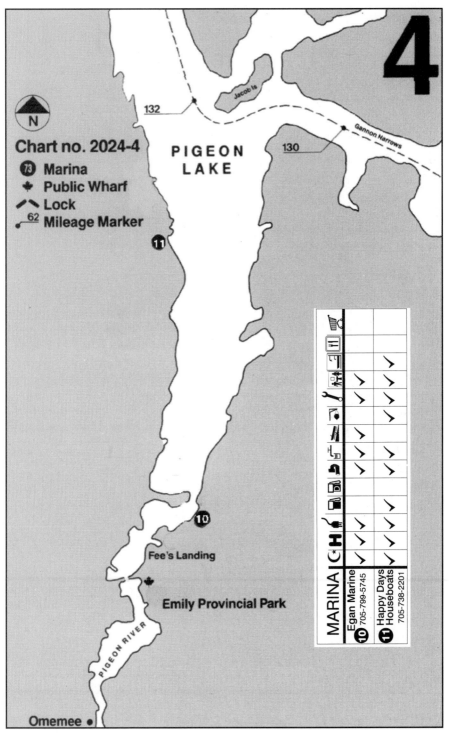

4

Jacob Is

132

Gannon Narrows

130

PIGEON LAKE

N

Chart no. 2024-4

73 Marina
✚ Public Wharf
Lock
62 Mileage Marker

11

10

Fee's Landing

Emily Provincial Park

PIGEON RIVER

Omemee •

MARINA	⟲	⏚	⌁	⛽	🛒	🔌	🔧	🛏	⚙			
10 Egan Marine 705-799-5745	✓	✓	✓			✓	✓		✓	✓		✓
11 Happy Days Houseboats 705-738-2201	✓	✓	✓	✓			✓	✓	✓	✓	✓	✓

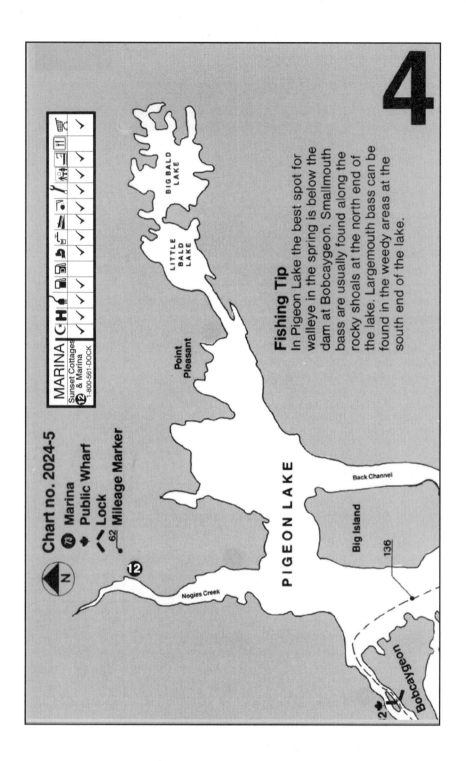

Fishing Tip

In Pigeon Lake the best spot for walleye in the spring is below the dam at Bobcaygeon. Smallmouth bass are usually found along the rocky shoals at the north end of the lake. Largemouth bass can be found in the weedy areas at the south end of the lake.

Chart no. 2024-5

73 Marina
♦ Public Wharf
Lock
62 Mileage Marker

N

MARINA

Sunset Cottages & Marina
1-800-561-DOCK

BIG BALD LAKE
LITTLE BALD LAKE
Point Pleasant
PIGEON LAKE
Back Channel
Big Island
136
Nogies Creek
Bobcaygeon

4

Eganridge Inn & Country Club

On the north shore of Sturgeon Lake, this glorious inn and country club has been labeled 'an absolute knock out' by travel writers and has been awarded the AAA/CAA Four Diamond Award for its exceptional accommodations, upscale facilities, attentive service and high standard of hospitality.

Since 1988 John and Patti Egan have turned this log house and estate into the impressive Inn and Country Club it now is. It combines a nine hole golf course, marina, tennis courts, beach, and fine dining. The fine, yet casual, dining, prepared by Swiss-born and Swiss-trained chef Alfred Keller, is beyond compare, served in the elegant dining room, 'The Barn,' overlooking the panoramic vistas of the grounds and golf course. This is a golf course that is considered to be one of the most beautifully maintained, and challenging of its kind in Ontario. In addition to the main inn several cedar log chalets dot the property offering guests a commanding view of the manicured golf course and expansive Sturgeon Lake.

Eganridge offers an elegant, romantic getaway bathed in beauty and tranquility. You can dock your boat at Eganridge's marina and spend a glorious evening ashore in luxurious surroundings. A driving tour of the Kawarthas is not complete without a stay or a meal at this outstanding country inn. For more information see advertisement on page one of this guide.

Area

5

Lake

Scugog

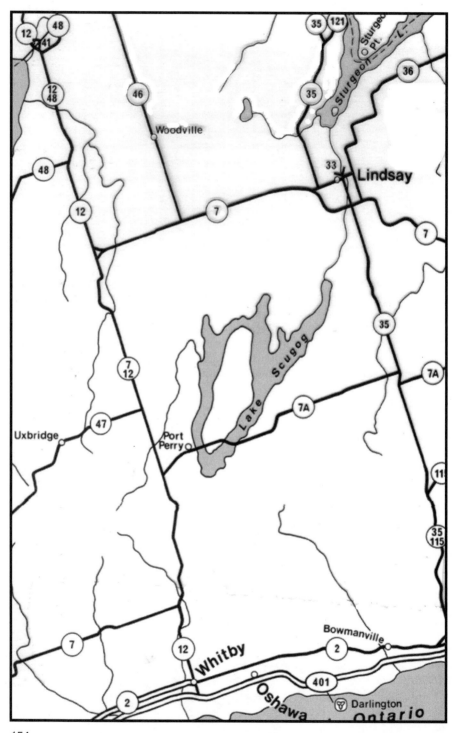

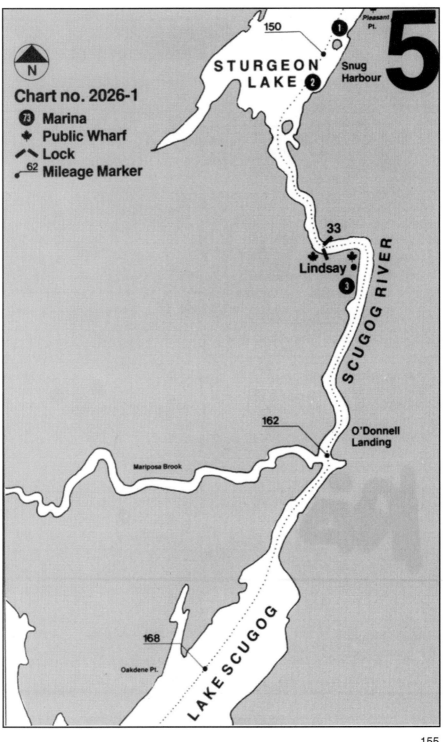

Chart no. 2026-1

N

🅐 Marina
♣ Public Wharf
⤬ Lock
•⁶² Mileage Marker

STURGEON LAKE

150

❶ Pleasant Pt.

Snug Harbour

❷

33

Lindsay

❸

SCUGOG RIVER

162

O'Donnell Landing

Mariposa Brook

168

Oakdene Pt.

LAKE SCUGOG

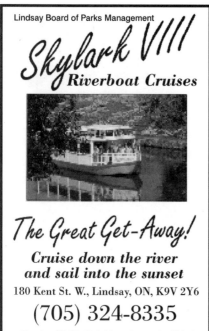
Navigation Note

The Scugog River is a narrow and weedy river. There are submerged stumps and deadheads close to the channel. Keep a close watch when proceeding through the river.

Strong currents may occur below the Lindsay lock.

Chart no. 2026-1

MARINA	☪	H	🛥	🚤	🅿	⚓	🍺	🎣	🚩	🔧	🚻	🛏	🍴	🛒
The Moorings at Snug Harbour ❶ 705-324-6667	✓		✓	✓		✓	✓	✓	✓	✓	✓	✓		✓
Lunge Haven ❷ 705-324-6610	✓		✓	✓			✓	✓			✓	✓		✓
Rivera Park ❸ 705-324-2393	✓	✓	✓					✓			✓	✓		

Lindsay: Lock #33

The Rainbow Bridge, upstream from the lock, has a clearance of 11 feet/3.3 m. The 2 bridges downstream from the lock have clearances of 13.5 feet/4 m. This lock is unusual in that it has three gates. One gate makes the chamber 36 feet/11 m in length and the other makes the chamber 106 feet/28 m long. Depending on the size and number of boats locking through, the chamber size can be adjusted accordingly.

There is tie-up space on the lower reach only. Pickerel/walleye fishing is great in the spring when the dam is open and in October when the logs are being pulled from the dam.

It is approximately a 10 minute walk into the town of Lindsay.

What a trip!

Lindsay

●●●●●●●●●●●●●●●●●●

This site was originally called Purdy's Mills after William Purdy who dammed the Scugog River at the rapids and proceeded to establish a sawmill. The dam caused hundreds of acres of land upriver to flood, resulting in a near riot from fellow settlers. Purdy's irate neighbours destroyed his dam which he later replaced with a lower one. The dam still caused a 10 foot/3 m raise in the water level, much to everyone's chagrin, but the government stepped in on Purdy's behalf and the dam remained. Purdy then built a gristmill and the settlement grew. Its name was changed to Lindsay in memory of one Mr. Lindsay who was accidently shot while assisting John Huston in the original town survey. He died of complications resulting from this wound.

Known as the 'Gateway to the Kawartha Lakes', Lindsay lies on the Scugog River. Its 20,000 inhabitants are proud of their town and have good reason to be. Their very wide main street is lined with many fine shops, restaurants and boutiques to serve you. There are also 5 shopping malls, 2 at the west end of town and one at the north end, and two more in the downtown area. The Lindsay Art Gallery, featuring Canadian paintings, and the Victoria County Museum, are both located on Kent Street. The museum has a rather unique display of 19th century glass and features an apothecary's shop, toy shop, general store and doctor's office from this period.

The Academy Theatre on Lindsay Street is home to the Kawartha Summer Theatre who takes to the stage with live professional theatre. As well the Academy Theatre hosts a variety of other live musical and theatrical special guests throughout the year including Tommy Hunter, Ian Tyson, Liona Boyd, John McDermott Call (705)324-9111 for information.

If you feel the need for a little exercise, you might want to take advantage of Lindsay's excellent golf courses, tennis and squash facilities or its indoor swimming pool. Of its many parks, Victoria Park (1) on Kent Street holds a number of outdoor concerts during the summer., McDonnell Park (2), just steps from the Academy Theatre (3), has beautiful floral displays and day-use docking and Rivera Park (4) has overnight docking. Rivera Park has water and electricity, showers, picnic facilities and playground and is just a short walk from downtown shopping.

Lindsay hosts many special events during the summer. Of particular interest are the Antique Show & Sale at the Victoria Park Armoury in mid-July, the River Festival Celebrations on the last weekend of July and the Lindsay Central Exhibition during the third week of September, the Historical Society Annual Garden Tour and the Christmas House Tour. Conklin's World's Finest Shows awarded Lindsay's fair the Best Overall Entertainment Fair in Ontario winning from among about 100 other fairs and exhibitions across the province. It draws over 40,000 visitors annually. You can get to Lindsay on Hwys 7, 35 and 36.

LINDSAY!

The perfect place to play....

Whether you want to fill your days with activities
or just sit back and enjoy the scenery,
Lindsay has everything you're looking for.

Call or write the Chamber at:
2 Kent St. W., Lindsay, Ontario K9V 2Y1
(705) 324-2393 Fax (705) 324-2473
e-mail: coc@lindsaytown.org

A leisurely cruise down the Scugog River will bring waterway visitors to Lake Scugog. The channel bends around Scugog Island heading south to the historic village of Port Perry well known for its Victorian main street. There are marina facilities here to tend to visiting boaters needs.

Nearby Scugog Island now boasts a new gambling centre called the Great Blue Heron Charitable Casino. Visitors to Scugog Island Marina can make arrangements to get to the casino from there as well as from Port Perry. It is located on Scugog Island Road.

THE TOWN OF

LINDSAY

PRESENTS

"The Lazy Days of Summer"

STARRING

KAWARTHA *Summer* **Theatre** ③

LIVE PROFESSIONAL THEATRE

"COME AS YOU ARE - SHORTS, SANDALS OR SWEATS"

2 LINDSAY ST. S. **705-324-9114**

Take in a Matinee or Evening Performance During July & August

TREAT YOURSELF TO TERRIFIC DINING & SHOPPING BEFORE OR AFTER THE SHOW!

⑦ **Deirdre's**
Fashions & Accessories

MARY ROSE • NORMA PETERSON
GLENSPORT TRAVEL

138 Kent St. W.   **705-328-2789**

⑧ **THE NUTTY CHOCOLATIER** CO. LTD.
OLDE FASHIONED CANDY & ICE CREAM STORE

"GO AHEAD...INDULGE YOURSELF"
3 Kent St. W.   **705-878-3451**

⑥ **OLYMPIA RESTAURANT**

ECLECTIC MEDITERRANEAN ATMOSPHERE
*Dine al fresco on the patio or
in air conditioned comfort*

106 Kent St. W.   **705-328-1444**

⑤ *The Winchester Arms*
:*"Your Friendly British Pub"*
47-49 William St. N.   **705-878-4312**

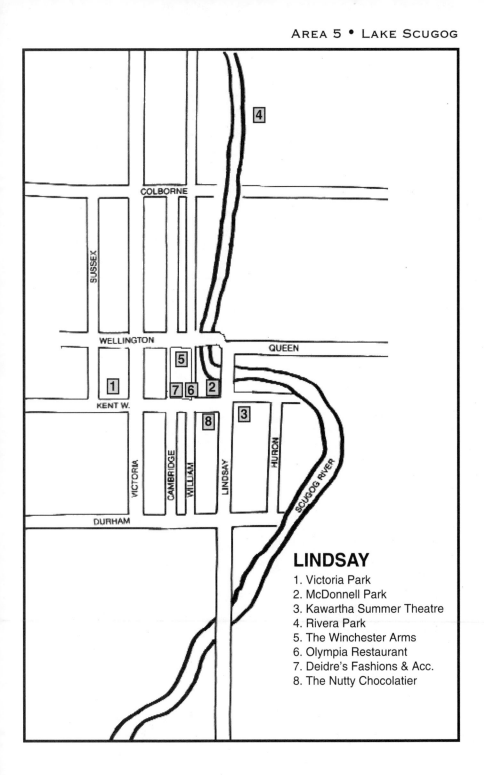

LINDSAY

1. Victoria Park
2. McDonnell Park
3. Kawartha Summer Theatre
4. Rivera Park
5. The Winchester Arms
6. Olympia Restaurant
7. Deidre's Fashions & Acc.
8. The Nutty Chocolatier

Chart no. 2026-2

MARINA	☾	H	⛽	⛽	⛽	⚓	🚿	⛴	🛟	🔧	🚻	🛏	🍴	🛒
5 Goreski's Lakeside Recreation 905-985-9763	✓	✓	✓	✓		✓	✓	✓	✓	✓	✓	✓	✓	
6 Port Perry Marina 905-985-3236	✓		✓	✓		✓	✓	✓		✓	✓	✓	✓	✓
7 West Shore Marine 905-985-2658-	✓	✓	✓	✓		✓	✓	✓	✓	✓	✓	✓	✓	

The Great Blue Heron Charitable Casino

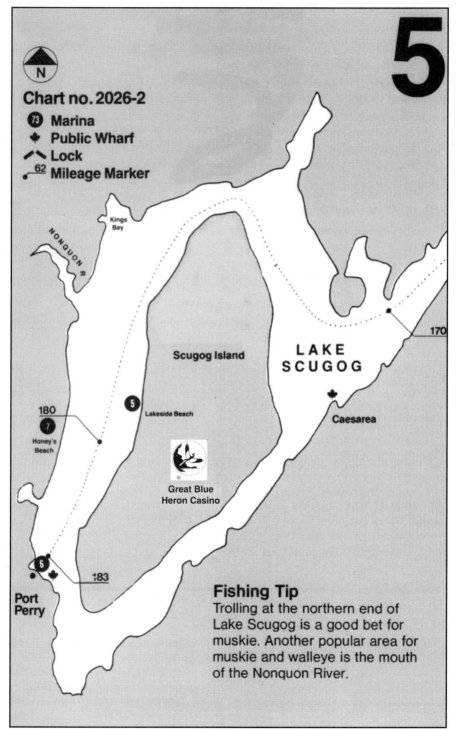

Chart no. 2026-2

🕖 Marina
✚ Public Wharf
⌒ Lock
•⁶² Mileage Marker

NONQUON R.

Kings Bay

Scugog Island

L A K E
S C U G O G

Lakeside Beach

170

180
🕖
Honey's
Beach

5

Caesarea

Great Blue
Heron Casino

6
183

Port
Perry

Fishing Tip
Trolling at the northern end of
Lake Scugog is a good bet for
muskie. Another popular area for
muskie and walleye is the mouth
of the Nonquon River.

Port Perry

•••••••••••••••••••

The first settlers in this area, at the south-west end of Lake Scugog, were Charles and Elias Williams. They sold a tract of their land to Peter Perry, who was instrumental in laying out the plans for a village here. Prior to this, Purdy's Mill had been built downriver at what is now Lindsay and because of this, the water level rose 10 feet/3 m thereby flooding the low-lying farmland and considerably altering the shoreline of the Scugog River. Although the flooding wreaked havoc, it later gave larger vessels access to the village. Mills were built at "Scugog Village" in 1846 and the village played an important role in the lumber trade as a trans-shipment point. Scugog Village was renamed Port Perry in 1852.

Port Perry was the birthplace of D.D. Palmer, the founder of chiropractic. It is a little known fact that Palmer was a Canadian from Port Perry and that this drugless practitioner defined the basics of the science. Palmer Park on the waterfront has a statue and a plaque to commemorate him.

Port Perry is an interesting town with pleasant old homes and an attractive lakeside setting. The Victorian main street features over 100 unique stores and services. In addition to family restaurants and small cafes, are laundromats, banks, a post office, liquor and beer stores.

Among the annual events held in Port Perry is the Canoe the Nonquon Race on the first Saturday of June. Port Perry's Canada Day celebrations include a Beef BBQ in Palmer Park prior to an exciting fireworks display that can be enjoyed from boat or land. During the summer season, Concerts in the Park are a regular Sunday afternoon attraction. Festival Days are usually held on the 2nd weekend of July and the Port Perry Fair is on Labour Day weekend. Port Perry is located at the junction of Hwys 7, 7a, 12.

Also of interest is the Scugog Shores Museum on Scugog Island. It is comprised of 5 buildings and contains artifacts and exhibits of both native and pioneer life. There is a fully restored general store, a Methodist Church and a school house dating from 1880. Annual events include Pioneer Days held the 3rd weekend of June, as well as Fall Harvest Days in September. While on the island be sure to partake in the action at the new Great Blue Heron Charitable Casino. Arrangements can be made to get there from the village of Port Perry and marinas nearby. It is located on Scugog Island Road.

Enjoy a leisurely cruise down the Scugog River and *Discover* beautiful Lake Scugog and historic Port Perry.

"You'll be glad you did!"

Township of Scugog

P.O. Box 780
Port Perry, Ontario L9L 1A7
For information please call
1-905-985-7346

It's happening!

THE SHORES OF LAKE SCUGOG

Travel Notes

●●●●●●●●●●●●●●●●●●

Area

6

Bobcaygeon to Lake Simcoe

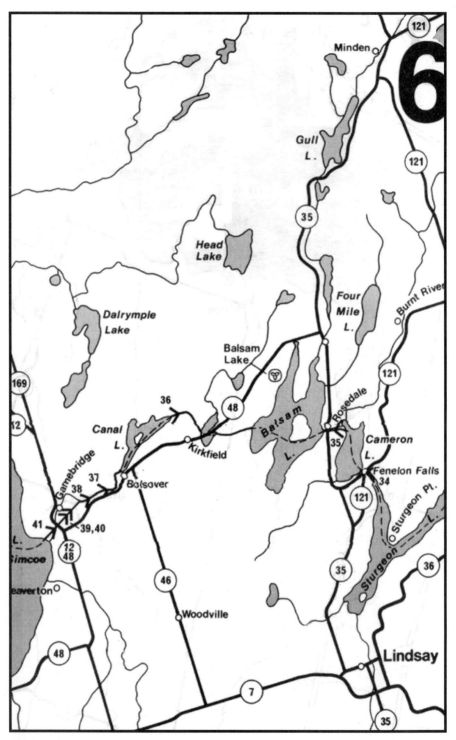

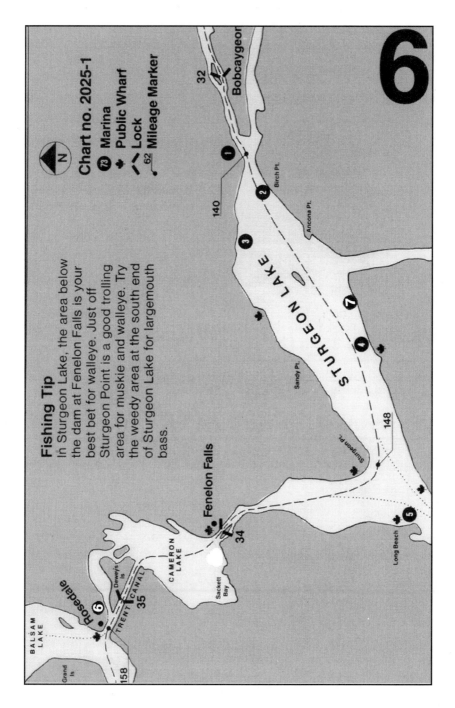

6

Chart no. 2025-1

70 Marina
+ Public Wharf
✚ Lock
62 Mileage Marker

N

Fishing Tip

In Sturgeon Lake, the area below the dam at Fenelon Falls is your best bet for walleye. Just off Sturgeon Point is a good trolling area for muskie and walleye. Try the weedy area at the south end of Sturgeon Lake for largemouth bass.

Bobcaygeon

Birch Pt.

Ancona Pt.

STURGEON LAKE

Sandy Pt.

Sturgeon Pt.

Fenelon Falls

Long Beach

CAMERON LAKE

Sackett Bay

Dewey's Is

TRENT CANAL

Rosedale

BALSAM LAKE

Grand Is

Chart no. 2025-1

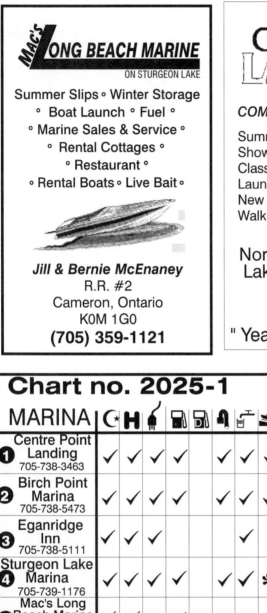

MARINA	☪	H		⚡	⛽	⛽		🥤			🔧	🚻	🛏	🍴	🛒
1 Centre Point Landing 705-738-3463	✓	✓	✓	✓		✓	✓	✓	✓	✓	✓	✓	✓	✓	
2 Birch Point Marina 705-738-5473	✓	✓	✓	✓		✓	✓	✓	✓	✓	✓	✓			
3 Eganridge Inn 705-738-5111	✓	✓	✓				✓				✓	✓	✓		
4 Sturgeon Lake Marina 705-739-1176	✓	✓	✓	✓		✓	✓	✳		✓	✓	✓			
5 Mac's Long Beach Marina 705-359-1121	✓	✓		✓			✓			✓	✓		✓		
6 Rosedale Marina 705-887-1663	✓	✓	✓	✓		✓	✓	✓	✓	✓	✓	✓			✓
7 McLaren's Marina 705-793-2280	✓		✓	✓		✓	✓	✓	✓	✓	✓	✓	✓		

Fenelon Falls

●●●●●●●●●●●●●●●●●●

Three of the first settlers in this area were John Langton of England who bought 500 acres and James Wallis of Ireland who acquired lands in partnership with Robert Jameson. Wallis and Jameson erected a sawmill and gristmill around 1834 and the settlement grew from there. Wallis, who is generally considered the founder of Fenelon Falls, encouraged settlement and donated land for the community's first church. He conducted the services himself until a clergyman arrived to do the job in 1838.

In 1877, the government completed 2 flight locks at the falls and these were replaced by one new electric lock between 1961 and 1963. The lock has a lift of 24 feet/7.3 m from Sturgeon Lake into Cameron Lake. Take in the spectacular falls, while at the locks, the result of a 7 foot/2.5 m drop rushing over the limestone gorge.

While you are in town browsing, why not pay a visit to James Wallis' house, now home to Mayboro Lodge Museum/Fenelon Falls Museum at 50 Oak Street. Originally built in 1837 by James Wallis, this was the first house in town. It is now completely restored and contains many pioneer and Indian artifacts of the mid 1800s. It is open daily from June to September. In town there are many stores, boutiques and restaurants to serve you. You will find a detailed account of town amenities on the following page.

The Fenelon Falls Agricultural Fair is usually held in mid August. There is also a Home and Recreation Show in May and Lobsterfest at the Curling Club in June. See the Fairs and Festivals guide for details.

Fenelon Falls: Lock #34

Over 300,000 visitors come to this lock to watch the boats lock through. The lock staff are constantly in public view and have to perform a new show every 30 minutes. Because this is such a busy lock, a strict policy is maintained forbidding any boats, other than those locking through, to tie up at the blue line. If the area beyond the blue line is full, rafting off is suggested. There is docking at the railway bridge upstream from the lock and staff can advise you of alternative docking facilities. A video camera monitors activities on the lower reach of the lock. The lock is busiest during mid-afternoon.

Around & About Fenelon Falls...

1. Dockside Grill
Wings, Burgers, Steaks,
Nachos & Much More–LLBO
12 Water St. 887-6983

2. The Livery Stable
Gifts, Ladies, Men's
& Children's Wear
4 May St. 887-3065

3. The Country Cupboard
Specialty Foods N Things
Featuring Frozen Yogurt
in Waffle Cones
9 May Street 887-6644

4. Kathy's Pet Foods
Dog Training, Dog Grooming
Pet Foods & Accessories
4-B May Street 887-5467
(behind the Livery Stable at the Locks)

5. Trail and Street
Footwear for your Lifestyle
16 May Street 887-6911

6. Twenty May Street
Quality Clothes & Accessories
20 May St. 887-2220

Victorian Bed & Breakfasts

7. The Rhubarb Patch
20 Oak St. 887-9586

8. The Olde Rectory
54 Louisa 887-9796

9. Sneakers Etc.
Nike, Reebok, Sandals,
Canvas & Water Shoes
Other Family Footwear
3 Francis St. W. 887-1100

10. Shutterbug Photofinishing
Cameras, Batteries, Film
Frames & Accessories
Enlargements & Fax Service
3 Francis St. W. 887-5808

11. Fenelon Cleaners & Laundromat
Wash & Fold Service, Alterations & Repairs
16 Market St 887-2472

12. Stinson Pharmacy
Beauty Aids &
Pharmaceuticals
53 Colborne St 887-2320

13. Fenelon Pet Supplies
Pet Food & Accessories
51 Colborne St. 887-6859

BOWES & COCKS LIMITED *The Gallery of Homes* REALTOR
14.
29 Colborne St.
887-3180
1-800-241-0667

PICK N' SAVE
15. Pick N' Save
Toys, Houseware,
Linen, Crafts & Yarn
27 Colborne Street
887-2641

16. Chelsea Bun Bakery
Specializing in Novelty,
All Occasion Cakes &
Fresh Baked Goods
25 Colborne St. 887-3400

17. Sunshine Freshmart
Good old fashioned, friendly service
with over 100 new products at lower prices.
48 Colborne St.

Fenelon Falls

18. **Purse Strings**
Consignment Clothing

Village Barber Shop
42 Colborne St   887-9645.
(at the lights)

21. **Stokes on Trent**
Jewellery, China, Gifts
Souvenirs & Repairs
8-10 Colborne St.   887-2930

24. **Taggart's Landing Restaurant**
Affordable Dining
Relaxed Atmosphere
Minutes From Locks
887-9000

19. **The Bookfinder**
Rare, Scarce & Used Books
In Hardcover & Paperback
Bought & Sold
Colborne Street   887-5052

22. **Canadian Tire Store**
For all your Marine &
Boating Supplies
Hwy. 121 887-3310

24. **Fenelon Inn**
Luxury Accommodations
Reasonably Priced
Great Location
887-9000

20. **Fenelon Falls IGA**
The Friendly Supermarket
Colborne St.
Across from the Locks

23. **Sundial Motel & Restaurant**
Open 7a.m. for Breakfast
Home Baked Goods
157 Lindsay St.   887-2400

25. **Forster's Antiques & Collectibles**
Hwy 121 Just North of Town
887-4134

Rosedale

●●●●●●●●●●●●●●●●●●●

Lock 35 at Rosedale, lifts crafts the final 4 feet/1.25 m from Cameron Lake to Balsam Lake. Balsam Lake has the highest elevation on the Trent-Severn Waterway.

Rosedale is a scenic and friendly little community that takes great pride in its role as one of the busiest locks on the waterway. There are 2 churches and a number of marinas in this hamlet as well as plentiful accommodation. You will also find everything you might need in the way of groceries, ice, tackle and bait. The lock grounds here have fine picnic facilities. Rosedale can be found by car on Hwy 35.

Rosedale: Lock #35

This lock is one of the busiest locks on the waterway. Often during peak weekends more than 50 boats tie up at this lock.

The spacious parkland at the lock has barbecues and about 20 picnic tables. The lock is fairly shallow, with a 4 foot/1.25 m lift and the average lock-through time is about 15 minutes.

Rosedale, Lock 35

Chart no. 2025-2

MARINA	☾	H	🔌	⛽	🛢	🔧	🚰	🛥	🅿	🔧	🚻	🛏	🍴	🛒
6 Rosedale Marina 705-887-1663	✓	✓	✓	✓		✓	✓	✓	✓	✓	✓	✓		✓
8 Nahma Lodge Marina 705-887-3309	✓			✓		✓	✓	✓	✓	✓	✓			✓
11 Thompson's Marina 705-454-3372	✓	✓	✓	✓		✓	✓	✓	✓	✓	✓			

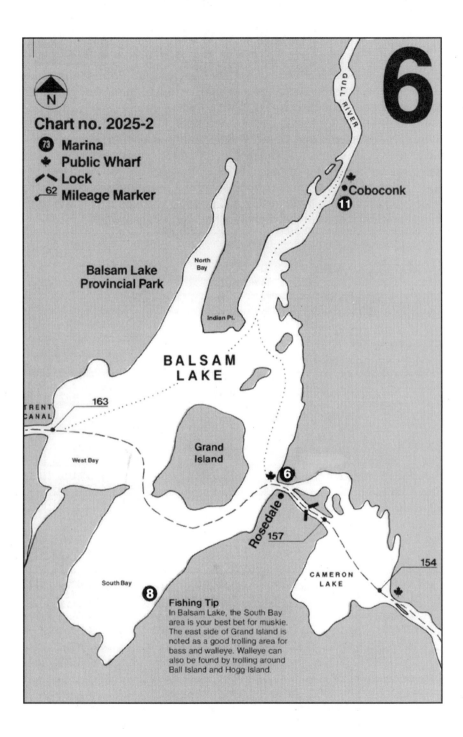

Chart no. 2025-2

- **73** Marina
- Public Wharf
- Lock
- _62_ Mileage Marker

GULL RIVER

Coboconk

11

Balsam Lake
Provincial Park

North
Bay

Indian Pt.

**BALSAM
LAKE**

TRENT
CANAL

163

West Bay

Grand
Island

6

Rosedale

157

CAMERON
LAKE

154

South Bay

8

Fishing Tip
In Balsam Lake, the South Bay
area is your best bet for muskie.
The east side of Grand Island is
noted as a good trolling area for
bass and walleye. Walleye can
also be found by trolling around
Ball Island and Hogg Island.

176

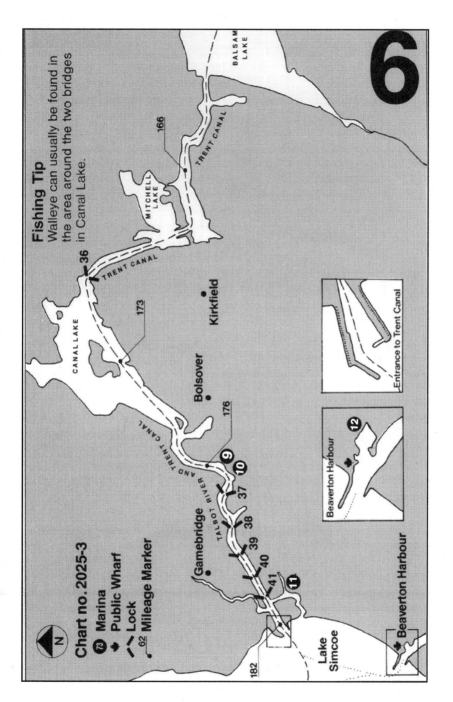

Chart no. 2025-3

🅜 Marina
✦ Public Wharf
⟋ Lock
62 Mileage Marker

Fishing Tip
Walleye can usually be found in the area around the two bridges in Canal Lake.

BALSAM LAKE

TRENT CANAL

166

MITCHELL LAKE

36

TRENT CANAL

173

CANAL LAKE

Kirkfield

Bolsover

176

TALBOT RIVER AND TRENT CANAL

9

10

37

38

39

40

41

11

Gamebridge

182

Lake Simcoe

Entrance to Trent Canal

Beaverton Harbour

12

Beaverton Harbour

177

Navigation Note

Balsam Lake is a deep water lake and is a good area for cruising.

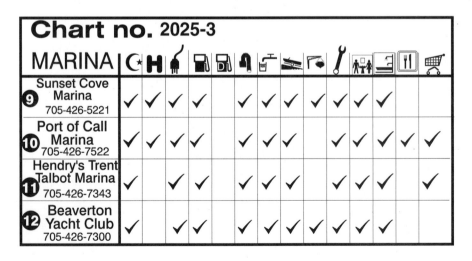

Chart no. 2025-3

MARINA	C*	H	🔌	⛽	⛽	⚓	🚰	ramp	flag	🔧	👪	🛏	🍴	🛒
9 Sunset Cove Marina 705-426-5221	✓	✓	✓	✓		✓	✓	✓	✓	✓	✓			
10 Port of Call Marina 705-426-7522	✓	✓	✓	✓		✓	✓	✓		✓	✓	✓	✓	✓
11 Hendry's Trent Talbot Marina 705-426-7343	✓		✓	✓		✓	✓	✓		✓	✓	✓		✓
12 Beaverton Yacht Club 705-426-7300	✓		✓	✓		✓	✓	✓	✓	✓	✓			

Balsam Lake Provincial Park

●●●●●●●●●●●●●●●●●●

L ocated on the west shore of North Bay, just off Hwy 48, this is a large recreational park which attracts many boaters and motorists each summer. There are hundreds of tent and trailer sites here, a few of which have electrical hook-ups. The park has a picnic area, washrooms, showers and laundry facilities.

A large safe beach is located in the day-use area of the park and there is a playground in the campgrounds. A self-guided trail is located in the park interior and it runs 1.5 miles/2.5 km through varying terrain. Ask for a self-guided pamphlet to take along on this 1.5 hour trek through the woods. Call (705) 454-3324 for information.

A lazy Trent-Severn afternoon

Coboconk

●●●●●●●●●●●●●●●●●●

"The Friendly Village", just north of Rosedale at Hwys 35 and 48, is located on the east side of Balsam Lake. The village has antiques, gift and craft shops for your browsing pleasure. Other services include a marina, hardware, liquor and beer store, laundromat, instant-teller, grocery store, pharmacy, medical centre, restaurants and churches. The updated town docks are within walking distance to all of these amenities. Coboconk also has 2 public parks and a public beach, with washrooms and a playground. A tourist information centre is located on the main street.

Local historical sites in the area include the Pattie House Hotel on Main Street, and Ye Olde Jailhouse, now a Seniors' craft shop, next to the Marina. Be sure to check out the restoration of Coboconk's Railway station which was recently saved and moved to legion park. A picturesque waterfall just south of the town docks on Main Street makes a lovely setting for photographs.

The Coboconk Lions Festival Weekend the third weekend in July and the Coby Family Games Day in early August both feature many activities and plenty of entertainment. Special events at the Royal Canadian Legion and the Coboconk Lions Community Centre are held throughout the year. Check the fairs and festivals guide for other activities or contact Victoria County Tourism (addresses and numbers can be found in the travel information section at the back of this guide).

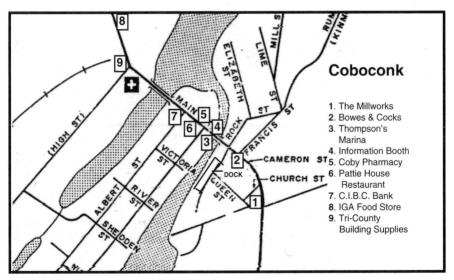

Coboconk

1. The Millworks
2. Bowes & Cocks
3. Thompson's Marina
4. Information Booth
5. Coby Pharmacy
6. Pattie House Restaurant
7. C.I.B.C. Bank
8. IGA Food Store
9. Tri-County Building Supplies

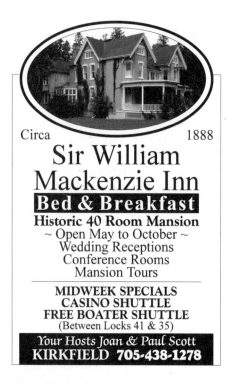
Navigation Note

Mitchell Lake and Canal Lake should be navigated with care because of submerged stumps and floating deadheads.

It is at the Kirkfield Lift Lock that the direction changes from upstream to downstream. Make a note of the buoy positions after passing through the lock.

The Historic Sir William Mackenzie Inn, Kirkfield

Kirkfield

● ● ● ● ● ● ● ● ● ● ● ● ● ● ● ● ● ● ●

The hydraulic lift lock at Kirkfield is the 2nd highest lock in North America and will lower you 49 feet/15 m in the Trent Canal as you begin your decent to Georgian Bay. This is the watershed. From here to Port Severn the waters flow to Georgian Bay, so you will have to keep in mind that the buoys are reversed.

The Village of Kirkfield is about 1.8 miles/3 km south of the lift lock. It is here that Sir William Mackenzie co-founder of the Canadian Northern Railway and many other major Canadian corporations made his home until his passing in 1923. The Sir William Mackenzie home built in the late 1880s is now operating as a bed and breakfast known as the Sir William Mackenzie Inn. The 40 room mansion was purchased by Joan and Paul Scott in 1992 and has been lovingly restored. The Inn sits on picturesque grounds that can be viewed fromthe spacious verandah or any of the 7 large rooms with ensuite baths that are for guest accommodation. The site now occupies 13 acres but during it's heyday the Mackenzie estate consisted of 1,200 acres. In 1995 a tornado hit the grounds and over 100 stately trees were felled. From this devastation has come a unique Sculpture Garden which has nine wonderful works at present and more planned for the future. The Inn offers boaters a great opportunity to spend a night ashore. If that's not in the schedule, Inn tours can be arranged for groups of four or more at a modest $5 for adults and $3 for children. Make the Sir William Mackenzie your home base while exploring all that Kirkfield and immediate area have to offer.

The Carden Plain boasts many rare and endangered species for bird watchers. Golf, horseback riding and fishing are all available. The whole family can enjoy mini golf and go karting on the fastest quarter mile track in Ontario. You will find lots of antique shops too. The Old Tin House, on the outskirts of town, houses "The Estate"Flowers and Things. This makes an interesting stop for gardeners and craft enthusiasts to view the gardens and products both live and dried. Kirkfield is an active community with many special events. Keep Saturday of the Labour Day Weekend open and attend the annual Kirkfield Festival. A great family day featuring a fun centre, parade, art on the lawn, entertainment, antique cars, afternoon tea, crafts show, lots of food and much more. Kirkfield is located on Hwy 48 between Gamebridge and Coboconk.

Kirkfield Lift Lock: Lock #36

Boats coming too fast into the lock area from the east side cause a turbulent condition which delays opening the gates. It is important here to look for direction lights with arrows which point to the chamber that is being loaded. Proceed to tie up at the blue line on the side indicated by the direction lights. Boaters are asked to stay on board and have passes ready for attendants in order to expedite passage.

Strong wind conditions on the upper chamber can be difficult for houseboats.

Be sure to stop here and visit the Friends of the Trent-Severn Waterway gift shop. It is accommodated in an old Lockmaster's Watch House which was restored by FTSW volunteers over a 3 year period and moved to the Kirkfield site in 1995. The watch house dates back to the 1920s.

Lockmaster's Watch House

Kirkfield Liftlock

Bolsover/Gamebridge

● ● ● ● ● ● ● ● ● ● ● ● ● ● ● ● ● ●

This section along the Talbot River was originally the portage between Balsam Lake and Lake Simcoe. Much of this portage was incorporated into the Portage Road which was one of the Colonization Roads created to induce settlement in the northern hinterlands of Upper Canada.

There are 5 locks in the area between Canal Lake and Lake Simcoe. Although the canal along this section is only 4 miles/6.5 kms long, the combined elevation from Gamebridge lock 41 to Bolsover lock 37 is 75 feet/23 m. There are several marinas and good camping sites along this stretch as boaters often moor for the night before setting course to Lake Simcoe.

The marinas from Bolsover to Gamebridge can supply you with gas, pump-outs, repairs, groceries, ice and tackle and there are also motel accommodations in the area.

The waters just downstream from lock 38 are popular haunts for anglers interested in pickerel. You can reach Gamebridge on Hwy 12 from Port Perry or Hwy 48 from Beaverton.

Bolsover: Lock #37

This lock, situated near the small village of Bolsover, is the deepest, all-manual lock on the system with a lift of 22 feet/6.7 m. Boaters should attend to their lines during the ascent due to the turbulence and tie securely to the blue line on the lower reach so as not to be washed away when the lock is emptied.

Boaters are asked to proceed slowly through this section to the next lock upstream to prevent wake damage.

The lock is becoming a favourite tie-up spot due to the friendly staff and good fishing; lots of bass, pickerel/walleye, muskie and pike.

Talbot: Lock #38

A favourite tie-up spot due to the quiet atmosphere and excellent fishing, lock 38 is home to the Talbot River Fish Sanctuary which is within walking distance from the lock station. From April to June, pickerel/walleye, bass, pike, and some muskellunge and suckers congregate below the dam for the annual spawn.

Lock 38 has a beautiful but small picnic area on the upper reach.

Portage: Lock #39

This lock, often referred to as the 'Jewel of the Canal', is quiet and peaceful. There are picnic tables at the lock.

Thorah: Lock #40

This lock is quiet with friendly lockstaff. The lock area is well landscaped and has picnic tables. The lock control building has washrooms.

Gamebridge: Lock #41

Be sure to check weather conditions before heading from here into Lake Simcoe. The lockstaff should be able to advise you on current conditions. The lock, which is manually operated, was completed in 1906 and the original concrete is still holding. Average lockthrough time is about 20 minutes. There is a launching ramp close by.

Canal Cut to Lake Simcoe

Area

7

Lake Simcoe and Couchiching

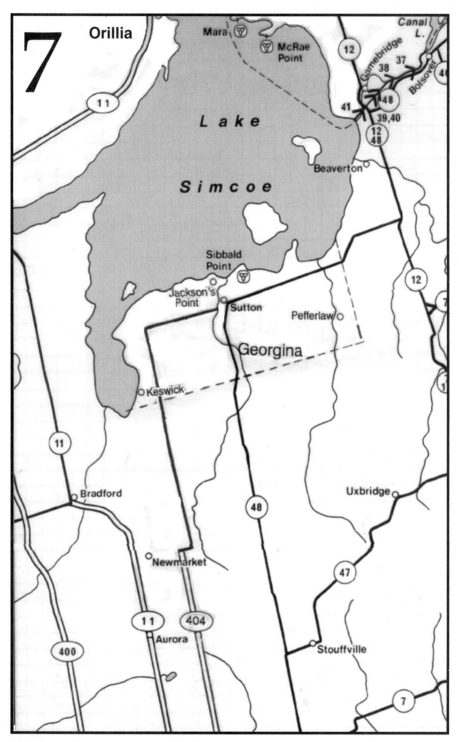

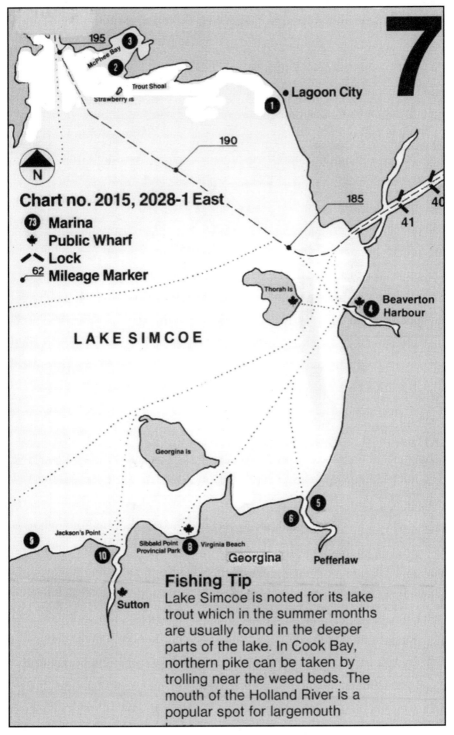

7

195

McPhee Bay

Trout Shoal

Strawberry is

190

N

Lagoon City

185

40

41

Chart no. 2015, 2028-1 East

🅰 Marina

♣ Public Wharf

⌃ Lock

•⁶² Mileage Marker

Thorah Is

Beaverton Harbour

L A K E S I M C O E

Georgina is

Jackson's Point

Sibbald Point Provincial Park

Virginia Beach

Georgina

Pefferlaw

Sutton

Fishing Tip

Lake Simcoe is noted for its lake trout which in the summer months are usually found in the deeper parts of the lake. In Cook Bay, northern pike can be taken by trolling near the weed beds. The mouth of the Holland River is a popular spot for largemouth

Lagoon City

Chart no. 2015, 2028-1E

MARINA	☾	H	⚡	⛽	⛽	🧊	🚰	🛥	⚓	🔧	👪	🛏	🍴	🛒
1 Lagoon City Marine Centre 705-484-5063-	✓		✓	✓	✓	✓	✓	✓	✓	✓	✓	✓	✓	✓
2 Marina Del Rey 705-325-3051	✓		✓			✓	✓		✓	✓	✓	✓	✓	
3 Starport Landing 705-325-3775	✓		✓	✓	✓	✓	✓	✓	✓	✓	✓	✓		✓
4 Beaverton Yacht Club 705-426-7300	✓		✓	✓		✓	✓	✓	✓	✓	✓	✓		
5 Flying Bridge Marina 705-437-2373	✓		✓	✓		✓	✓	✓	✓	✓	✓	✓	✓	
6 Everglades Marina 705-437-1340	✓		✓	✓		✓	✓	✓	✓	✓	✓	✓		
8 Virgina Beach Marina 705-437-2533	✓			✓		✓	✓	✓	✓	✓	✓		✓	
9 Mahoney's Marina 705-476-5463	✓		✓	✓			✓	✓		✓	✓		✓	
10 Bonnie Boats 705-722-3862	✳	✳	✳	✓			✓	✓		✓	✳		✳	✳

Lagoon City •••

L agoon City is situated on the eastern shore of Lake Simcoe, approximately 10 miles/16 kms north of Beaverton, off Highway 12. You will find the layout of this friendly urban town site very interesting with it's 8 miles /13 kms of interconnecting waterways that navigate through Lagoon City allowing you to cruise right up to your front door.

Visitors can enjoy a beautiful sandy beach, swimming, fishing, tennis, and dining at "Neptune's Bistro" overlooking the marina.

With easy access to Georgian Bay and the Trent-Severn Waterway, Lagoon City Marine Centre is an ideal home port for boating enthusiasts. Boaters are welcome at Lagoon City's excellent full service marine facilities where gas, diesel, pumpout and launch ramp are available. They offer seasonal and transient dockage, with 277 open and covered slips to accommodate boats up to 60 feet.

This is a beautiful waterfront community with a variety of activities for all ages...a warm welcome awaits you!

Beaverton

●●●●●●●●●●●●●●●●●●●●

L ocated 3 miles/5 kms south of the Trent-Severn, Beaverton is at the mouth of the Beaver River. A long concrete wharf greets visitors to the town together with 2 public boat launch ramps. The harbour area is best described as "quaint" with a number of picturesque and historic boat houses on the water together with parkland overlooking Simcoe.

A short walk from the harbour area is Beaverton's downtown featuring a wide range of goods and services from groceries, fine shops, and restaurants to accommodation, banking facilities, and a cinema. Nestled by the river is the Beaver River Museum. It is comprised of log cabins, the Old Stone Jail and other buildings open throughout the summer. Also available is the Beaverton Summer Arts Festival, live theatre from July 2nd to Labour Day, in the restored century old Town Hall. For more information contact the Township of Brock at (705) 432-2355.

Georgina

●●●●●●●●●●●●●●●●●●●

G eorgina's 32 miles/52 kms of waterfront, beaches, Provincial Parks and scenic routes offer a sparkling variety of recreational, social and cultural pursuits which keep its many guests entertained from sunrise to well after sunset. Lake Simcoe's clear blue waters provide swimming, sailing, windsurfing, waterskiing, scuba diving boating and fishing. The shoreline of Lake Simcoe is dotted with efficient marinas for your convenience. The Jackson's Point area bursts with activity in the summertime. It's a short 2.5 miles/4 kms west southwest of Sibbald's Point Provincial Park. There are 2 public wharves and a launching ramp. Nearby, enjoy an evening at the Red Barn Theatre (one of Canada's oldest theatres) after a quiet dinner overlooking Lake Simcoe at one of Georgina's fine resort restaurants.

On the southern tip of Lake Simcoe on the south-eastern shore of Cook's Bay is the progressive community of Keswick. There, a retail mall will service all your needs. Running through the centre of this community is the Jersey River, more commonly called the Maskinonge River.

The Pefferlaw River, on the easterly boundary of Georgina, provides a safe picturesque harbour for all types of boats. Don't forget about the winter, Georgina is known as the Ice Fishing Capital of Canada.

Bradford

• • • • • • • • • • • • • • • • •

In 1815, 150 Highland Scots arrived to settle this area. They had previously settled at Red River, Manitoba under the sponsorship of Lord Selkirk, but crop failure and opposition from the North West Company led them to abandon the Red River Settlement and relocate. The Auld Kirk, which was built in 1869, replaced the original church built by the relocated highlanders in 1823. Just south of Bradford is the Holland Marsh which today is one of Ontario's most productive agricultural areas.

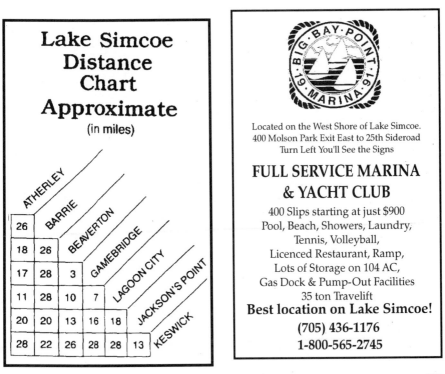

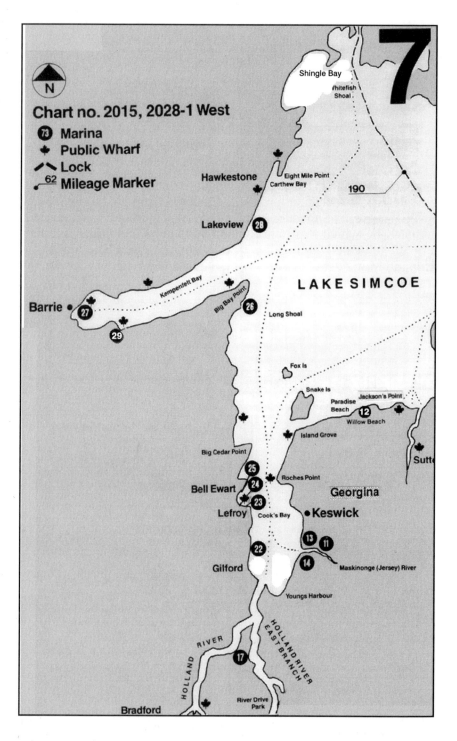

Chart no. 2015, 2028-1 West

73 Marina
Public Wharf
Lock
_62 Mileage Marker

Shingle Bay
Whitefish Shoal

Hawkestone
Eight Mile Point
Carthew Bay
190

Lakeview **28**

Kempenfelt Bay
Big Bay Point

LAKE SIMCOE

Barrie **27**
29
26
Long Shoal

Fox Is

Snake Is
Jackson's Point
Paradise Beach **12**
Willow Beach

Island Grove

Big Cedar Point

25
24
Roches Point

Bell Ewart
23
Lefroy   Cook's Bay   **Keswick**

Georgina

13 **11**
22
14
Gilford
Maskinonge (Jersey) River

Youngs Harbour

Sutt

HOLLAND RIVER

HOLLAND RIVER EASTBRANCH

17

River Drive Park
Bradford

Chart no. 2015, 2028-1W

MARINA	☾★	H	⚡	⛽	⛽	⚓	🚰	🛥	🚩	🔧	🚻	🛏	🍴	🛒
11 Keswick Marine 905-476-4343	✓		✓	✓		✓	✓	✓		✓	✓	✓	✓	✓
12 Mahoney's Marina 905-476-5463	✓		✓	✓		✓	✓			✓	✓		✓	
13 Crate Marine Sales 905-476-4321			✓			✓	✓	✓	✓	✓	✓			
14 Dawson's Marina Ltd. 705-739-1176	✓		✓	✓	✓	✓	✓	✓	✓	✓	✓			
17 Holland River Marina 705-853-6446	✓		✓	✓		✓	✓	✓	✓	✓	✓	✓		
18 Albert's Marina 705-836-4125	✓	✓	✓	✓	✓	✓	✓	✓	✓	✓	✓	✓	✓	✓
22 Kontiki Marina 705-456-2339	✓		✓			✓	✓		✓	✓	✓	✓	✓	
23 Lefroy Harbour Resorts 705-456-2120	✓		✓	✓	✓	✓	✓			✓	✓	✓	✓	
24 Monto Reno Marina Ltd. 705-456-3131	✓	✓	✓	✓		✓	✓	✓	✓	✓	✓	✓	✓	
25 Lake Simcoe Marine 705-456-3131	✓		✓				✓	✓	✓	✓	✓		✓	
26 Big Bay Point Marina 705-436-1176	✓	✓	✓	✓	✓	✓	✓	✓	✓	✓	✓	✓	✓	✓
27 City of Barrie Marina 705-739-4218	✓	✓	✓	✓		✓	✓	✓			✓	✓		
28 Gull Rock Marina Ent. 705-487-2850				✓			✓	✓		✓	✓	✓		
29 Brentwood Marine 705-722-8344			✓	✓		✓	✓			✓	✓	✓		

Barrie

● ● ● ● ● ● ● ● ● ● ● ● ● ● ● ● ● ●

To journey to Barrie by boat is to stumble upon one of Lake Simcoe's best kept secrets and you certainly won't be disappointed you came. Barrie has it all! Attractions! Events! Shopping! Dining! And Transient Docking!

Yes that's right! The City of Barrie is pleased to announce the planned expansion of it's transient docking facilities making it easier to access the beautiful waterfront parks and nostalgic downtown core. As you stroll the waterfront you will soon become aware of your close proximity to the many specialty shops as well as a wide array of dining opportunities and live entertainment. And if that isn't enough, why not enjoy one of the many festivals or events that make Barrie's waterfront such an enjoyable place to visit in the summer. Whether it be Kempenfest the 1st weekend in August, which is known as one of the largest outdoor arts and crafts festivals in North America, or Downtown Barrie's Promenade Days Street Festival the 1st week of July, there is always entertainment for all ages.

Should you decide to explore a little further inland, you will soon discover such treasures as Barrie's Golden Mile (a shopping Mecca), Molson Park (the ultimate concert venue), and the Barrie Molson Centre (home of the Barrie Colts and occasional host of such teams as the Toronto Raptors and Toronto Maple Leafs).

Barrie Marina

CITY OF BARRIE
MARINA

■ ■ ■   ■ ■ ■

Facilities:

- Dockage
- Gas / Oil / Ice
- Pump out
- Showers
- Fresh Water
- Hydro

Nearby Amenities:

- Hotels / Motels
- Restaurants
- Parks
- Groceries
- Cinemas
- Night Spots
- Shopping

DESTINATION:
Barrie
It's where we want you to be!

For more information call:
Stephen Harriman, Marina Co-ordinator
(705) 739-4218

So whether you have enjoyed a day on the sandy beach of Centennial Park or strolled through the shops of Downtown Barrie you will be promised that there is nothing as spectacular as the sunset that falls over the western end of Kempenfelt Bay and that beautiful waterfront city that 80,000 people call home...Barrie!

To book your boatslip please call the City of Barrie Marina at (705) 739-4218 (see advertisement for more details). For more information when making your plans to come to Barrie, please call the Barrie Visitor and Convention Bureau (705) 739-9444 or 1-800-668-9100.

Docking at Port of Orillia

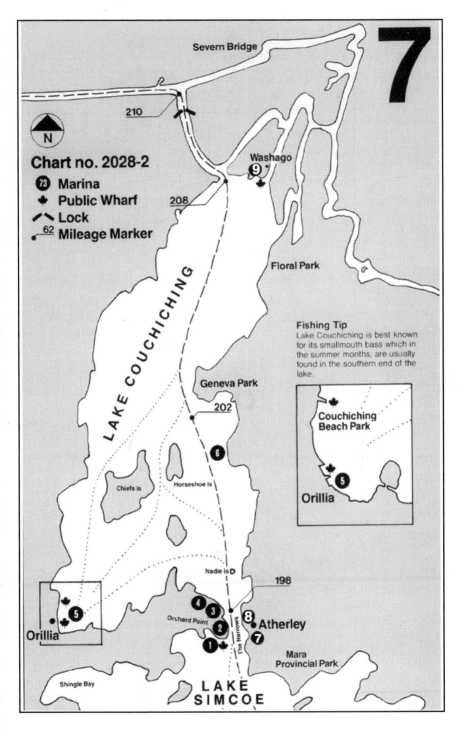

Severn Bridge

210

Chart no. 2028-2
73 Marina
🍁 Public Wharf
⋀ Lock
_62 Mileage Marker

Washago
9

208

Floral Park

LAKE COUCHICHING

Fishing Tip
Lake Couchiching is best known
for its smallmouth bass which in
the summer months, are usually
found in the southern end of the
lake.

Geneva Park

202

6

Couchiching
Beach Park

Chiefs Is

Horseshoe Is

5

Orillia

Nadie Is

198

5

Orillia

4 **3**

Orchard Point

8

2 **Atherley**

7

1

The Narrows

Mara
Provincial Park

Shingle Bay

**LAKE
SIMCOE**

Chart no. 2028-2

MARINA	☪	H	🔌	⛽	⛽	⚓	🚰	⛵	🚩	🔧	🚻	🛏	🍽	🛒
1 Orchard Point Marina 705-326-9413-				✓				✓	✓	✓				
2 Mariner's Pier 705-327-0251	✓	✓	✓	✓		✓	✓	✓		✓	✓	✓		✓
3 Mariposa Landing 705-326-7898	✓		✓			✓	✓		✓		✓	✓		
4 Hot Knots Landing 705-326-7898	✓	✓	✓	✓	✓	✓	✓	✓	✓	✓	✓	✓		✓
5 Port of Orillia 705-326-4424	✓	✓	✓			✓	✓		✓	✓	✓	✓	✓	✓
6 Ojibway Bay Marina 705-326-5855	✓		✓	✓	✓	✓	✓	✓	✓	✓	✓		✓	✱
7 Baer Harbour 705-325-2132	✓		✓				✓				✓	✓		
8 Blue Beacon 705-326-1145	✓		✓	✓		✓	✓	✓	✓	✓	✓		✓	
9 Shamrock Marina 705-689-2573	✓							✓	✓		✓	✓		

200

Mara Provincial Park

●●●●●●●●●●●●●●●●●●

S outh-east of Orillia, on the east shore of Lake Simcoe, lies Mara Provincial Park. The park has more than 100 campsites but no electrical hook-ups. There are toilets and picnic facilities at the park and a playground and swimming area. There is a boat launching ramp in the park and a boat rental nearby. By car Mara can be found just off Hwy 12 on County Road 44. For information phone (705) 326-4451.

Atherley Narrows Fish Weirs

●●●●●●●●●●●●●●●●●●●

T he fish weirs at Atherley Narrows were originally like an underwater fence that channeled fish to a specific opening.

Marine archeologists hoped to date these fish weirs back to 1615 coinciding with those mentioned in Champlain's journal. Champlain had written that the Huron closed almost the entire exit of the strait, where the big lake (Simcoe) emptied into the little lake (Couchiching), by using fish weirs. The Huron then netted the fish and preserved them for winter.

The archeologists sent some samples of the weir for radio carbon dating. To their surprise the samples were reported to be over 4,500 years old.

Orillia

●●●●●●●●●●●●●●●●●●●

Orillia has undergone many changes in the past few years. Its excellent waterfront facilities and lovely downtown shopping area have made it one of the most popular stops on the Trent-Severn Waterway.

As with many waterway towns, Orillia grew primarily because of the lumber industry which boomed in the mid 1800s. Once the timber stands were depleted and the lumber business slowed, agriculture came to the fore. By the turn of the century, Orillia had achieved a certain notoriety as a vacationland with abundant fishing grounds.

Today, Orillia is still a popular vacation town. Its Historical Main Streets feature a variety of restaurants, stores and boutiques. When on Mississaga Street be sure not to miss the old general store, the Mariposa Market. Wide, brick sidewalks, spotted with trees and benches give opportunity to relax and watch the local action.

The PORT OF ORILLIA is a transient marina located at the base of Mississaga Street. 222 slips are supplied with water and 30 amp service. Clean, newly renovated washrooms and showers are maintained by the Port's fully trained staff. Ice and vending machines are available at the Port Office. The Orillia and District Chamber of Commerce (705-326-4424), hosts many special events during the summer season at the Port of Orillia. Just next to the Port are Centennial and Couchiching Beach Parks. Here you will find the aqua theatre, which is home to Sunday Evening Band Concerts and many other performances throughout the summer months. The playgrounds, Miniature Steam Train, ball diamond and 1909 band shell complement the beautiful sandy beach, adding to your relaxing stay in Orillia.

If your are interested in live theatre, many fine productions are offered at the historical Orillia Opera House, located at the corner of Mississaga and West Streets. The box office can

inform you of upcoming shows (705-326-8011). On Saturday Mornings the colourful Farmers' Market is held directly behind the Opera House.

Orillia Boat Cruises offer cruises around Lake Couchiching and on the Severn River from May to October with daily morning and afternoon cruises, and dinner cruises with entertainment (705-325-2628).

They deal excitement at CASINO RAMA (1-888-817-7262). The size of two football fields, the casino boasts 109 gaming tables and 2,100 slot machines, a variety of restaurants and an entertainment lounge. The Casino is open 24 hours a day, 365 days a year. Many area hotels offer free shuttle service, and a free shuttle departs from downtown and the Port of Orillia.

Sir Sam Steele Art Gallery is located on Peter Street just right of Mississaga, the main street. It features a rare collection of Group of Seven paintings They are a real find to Gallery buffs.

The home of Canada's Famous humorist, Stephen Leacock Museum (705-329-1908), is located on the shores of scenic Lake Couchiching. His home remains much the way he left it. Leacock's letters, personal notes and the original, hand written manuscript of "Sunshine Sketches of a Little Town" are on display to the public.

Orillia the Golden

Spend a night ashore at
Betty & Tony's
Waterfront B & B
Docking for boats up to 45'.
Limo to town or Casino.
Central air. Private dining.
Paddle boat.

Atherley Narrows - West at
marker S 306

677 Broadview Avenue
Orillia, Ontario, L3V 6P1
Phone: **1 (800) 308-2579**
Email:tony.bridgens@encode.com
www.bbcanada.com/9.html
(member of the FOBBA)

B & B s

Bed & Breakfast guests are a special breed. Where many people opt into the uniformity of the chain hotels or motels, B & B people take a chance on the hospitality of unknown hosts in private homes of various kinds. They may have the opportunity of visiting with hosts, and finding out local lore, and certainly the experience is more personal than hotels. *Tony Bridgens*

Gord Souter's
HOUSEBOAT
VACATIONS

The possibilities are endless and it's tremendous value for the money. Spring and Fall vacations are an even better value. Fishing in the spring is excellent, and the beauty of the Trent-Severn Waterway in the fall is unbelievable. That's what separates houseboating from any other type of vacation--the freedom to choose your pace, to go where you want, when you want, and just relax, knowing you have all the comforts right with you.

An enjoyable vacation for the entire family
Located in Orillia
Reserve now (705)327-7591

- Full Breakfast
- TV in all bedrooms
- Fishing
- Welcome Snacks
- Non-Smoking Adults
- Swimming
- Boats Available
- Trasportaion to and from Casino Rama Available
- Dinner by Prior Arrangement
- BBQ
- Walking Distance to Tudhope Park and Restaurants
- Cross Country Skiing, Skating & Snowmobiling

FREE BOAT DOCKING
622 Moberley Avenue
Orillia, ON Canada L3V 6R6
Phone/Fax: **705-326-1636**

Stephen Leacock House Museum, Orillia

207

BIRDING IN AND AROUND ORILLIA

The Trent-Severn Waterway corridor offers 'birders' a tremendous variety of viewing opportunities whether aboard a boat or cruising in your land yacht. This article on Birding in and around Orillia was created by Greg Sadowski, owner of the Bird House Nature Company.

Bird watching is becoming a very popular pastime for many Canadians. It offers the serenity of nature and the challenge of finding and identifying the birds in your own backyard. Warblers, sparrows, hawks, ducks we've got them all right here in Orillia. Many species of birds can be observed at all times of the year. From the "rare ones" like the Northern Hawk Owl to the common American Robin, it's not hard to find them, you just have to know where to look. For a helping hand-there is the Orillia Naturalists Club which boasts some of the most knowledgeable people in Ontario, if not Canada, on the subject of birds. They would be more than happy to answer any questions you may have on Orillia's natural history.

Hot spots in the area include *The Uhthoff Recreational* Trail. It is managed by the local naturalist group and provides scheduled walks through its 11 km trail system. Here you may find hundreds of Spring migrants in May or visit the winter residents, Pine Grosbeaks or Great Gray Owls. Also, *Carden Plain*, east of Orillia, just north of Kirkfield, is a mix of farmland and woodland habitats and is part of the ecological transition taking place at the southern edge of the Canadian Shield. This habitat offers a variety of species including Loggerhead Shrikes and a number of shore birds. *Tiny Marsh* is a 567 hectare marsh approximately 40 minutes west of Orillia, by car. It is an excellent birding spot for nesting waterfowl and marsh species. The mature wooded areas along the trails are an excellent place to spot warblers. Viewing platforms are present here, as well as a boardwalk through the marsh. *Bass Lake Provincial Park*, just west of Orillia off of Hwy 12, has a small lake in which a number of waterfowl can be spotted. A maze of excellent trails take you through a variety of different habitats offering a great variety of bird species.

Whether you want to find a specific species or just see a variety of birds there are a great many places to visit. You won't be disappointed. So, come to Orillia and see the birds! To find out more information on these areas or about field guides and birding paraphernalia contact Greg Sadowski at *The Bird House Nature Company* (705)329-3939. The Orillia Naturalists Club can be reached at (705) 327-5177.

AT CASINO RAMA, IT'S ALWAYS SATURDAY NIGHT!

24 hours a day, every day of the year!

Get ready for the colour, music, laughter, food, dancing, lights and action of Casino Rama.

Over 2100 slot machines and more than 100 gaming tables. Three outstanding restaurants and a lounge

with live entertainment. Experience Casino Rama. Just like Saturday night, this place is always a party!

We Deal Excitement. BIG TIME.

Operated by
Carnival Hotels & Casinos

Rama, just off Highway 11, near Orillia **1-888-817-RAMA(7262) OR 1-705-329-3325**

Washago
● ● ● ● ● ● ● ● ● ● ● ● ● ● ● ● ● ●

In 1847, the construction of the Muskoka Road was undertaken. It was to run from Orillia to Washago and on to the Colonization Road which eventually ran north to Gravenhurst. The construction was a corduroy road, typical of that time. After the trail was cleared and levelled, logs were laid side by side across the road. It was bumpy at best and during spring thaw or heavy rains, many logs were upheaved, creating precarious, if not, hazardous travel. It did open the way for settlers, however, and a small settlement began at Washago primarily as a result of the lumber trade. In 1853, Quetten St. George established a large sawmill at Washago to accommodate timber being felled along Lake Couchiching.

Today Washago is basically a cottage community which has bakeries, restaurants, beer and liquor store, coin laundry and good accommodations. There is a public dock and a boat launching ramp here. Washago is located at the junction of Hwys 11 and 169.

Couchiching: Lock #42

Friendship Junction, as it is known by boaters, is another one of the busiest locks on the waterway. The lock staff feel that one of the important aspects of their work is to maintain good public relations with the boaters. Before heading into Lake Couchiching, you are advised to ask the lock staff about the weather conditions on the lake. You will be impressed with how adept the staff is at getting as many boats as possible into the lock chamber.

There is a grocery store and a restaurant within a short walk from the lock.

Navigation Note:

Be advised, the channel as you enter Sparrow Lake is shallow, stay between the markers. The water on the port side may be only 2 feet deep and is very rocky. Keep an eye out for danger markers.

Locking through at Lock 42, Couchiching.

Travel Notes

Area

Couchiching Lock to Port Severn

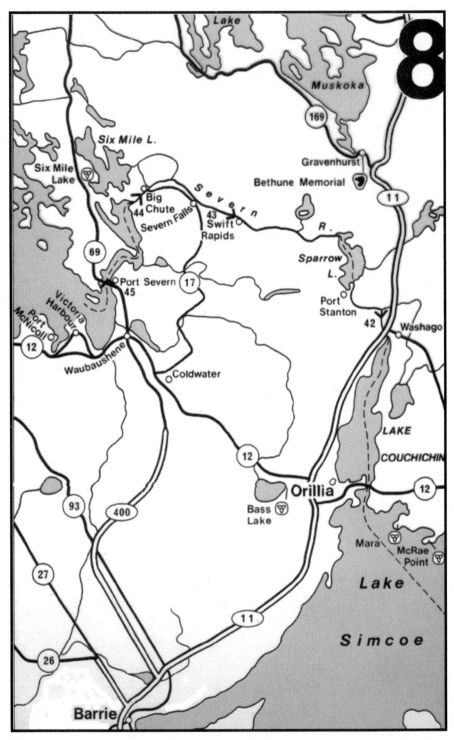

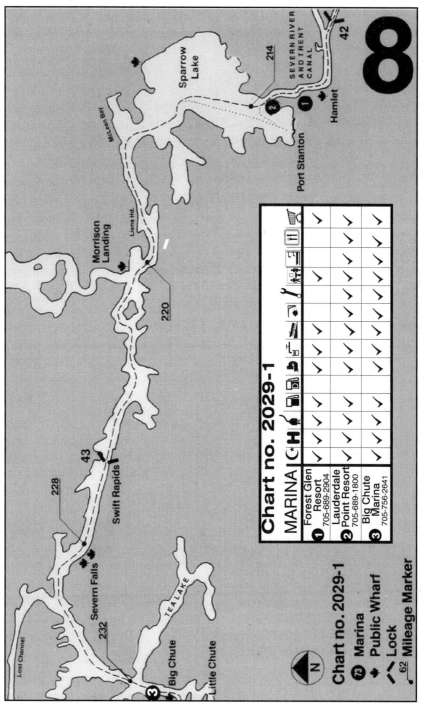

8

Sparrow Lake

McLean Bay

Morrison Landing

Lions Hd.

220

228

43

Swift Rapids

Severn Falls

232

Lost Channel

TEA LAKE

Big Chute

Little Chute

214

SEVERN RIVER AND TRENT CANAL

42

Hamlet

Port Stanton

Chart no. 2029-1

MARINA	🔌	⛽	📶	🛏	🔧	🚻	🍴	🛒
1 Forest Glen Resort 705-689-2904	✓ ✓ ✓	✓	✓	✓		✓		✓
2 Lauderdale Point Resort 705-689-1800	✓ ✓ ✓	✓	✓	✓	✓	✓	✓	✓
3 Big Chute Marina 705-756-2641	✓ ✓ ✓	✓	✓	✓	✓	✓	✓	✓

N

Chart no. 2029-1

🚤 Marina
🚩 Public Wharf
Lock
62 Mileage Marker

GREAT CASUAL DINING AT AFFORDABLE PRICES

Enjoy a quiet meal or drinks on Muskoka's only fully screened in patio offering a spectacular view of beautiful Sparrow Lake.

SILVER PINES RESTAURANT & SCREENED IN PATIO

(fully licensed by LLBO)

Kilworthy, Ontario **(705)689-2813**

Open nightly at 5:00 pm and all day Saturday and Sunday.
During July and August open at 11 a.m.

ASK ABOUT OUR SPECIALS.

Located in the North/East corner of Sparrow Lake
by the Government dock

"Great Memories, Great Adventures"

All the good things you remember about Ontario resorts...all summer long. Summer is for families at Bayview-Wildwood. We offer outdoor adventures, creative programs for children, and entertaining events each day, all in a family operated resort, close to home.

Supervised childrens' programs- Nightly family entertainment - Pool and Spa - Water-sports program- Horseback riding and pony rides - Hiking.

Stop in while moored at the Port Stanton Wharf. Only 10km north of Orillia on the south shore of Sparrow Lake in Port Stanton.

Call for reservations or information on our reasonable family packages:

1-888-422-9843

www.bayview.on.ca

Bayview-Wildwood Resorts,
RR1, Severn Bridge, ON, Canada P0E 1N0
Fax: (705) 689-8042

FOREST GLEN RESORT, R.R. #1, Severn Bridge, Ontario. P0E 1N0. **1-705-689-2904**. Your hosts: Vince and Terry Schweitzer. Self-catering cottages on the Trent-Severn Waterway at Hamlet Swing Bridge near Sparrow Lake. One and two bedroom cottages are fully equipped with modern conveniences, linens included. Horseshoe pits, evening campfires, playground, baseball, swimming, boating, fishing. Boat and motor rentals. General Store, live bait, gas, parking, docking, boat launching, Casino Rama& golf nearby.

May - October (store open year round)

Credit Cards Accepted

216

Port Stanton

●●●●●●●●●●●●●●●●●●

This resort area is located at the southern tip of Sparrow Lake. Captain Thomas Stanton arrived in Canada from England in 1862 and settled on the shores of Lake Couchiching. He married Ellen Franklin and worked as captain and engineer on steamboats plying Lake Couchiching and Lake Simcoe. The family moved to Sparrow Lake in 1875 where they cleared land and built their home. Captain Stanton was an enterprising fellow who began a steamship service on Sparrow Lake and had quite a fleet of ships over the years. After 1884, he built an inn to accommodate vacationers, anglers and hunters who visited the area during the summer. Over the years, this has developed into an entire complex of resort inns and cottages that are run by the Stanton family to this day. With the advent of the railway in 1906, Sparrow Lake was inundated with vacationers each summer.

Vacationers are still coming to Port Stanton to stay with the Stantons. Visitors can dock at the public wharf or park their cars near the dock. The store at the dock was started by Captain Stanton's son in 1901. There is a small beach at the dock and gas is available for boaters at the gas dock in front of the store. Bayview Wildwood Resort is located here and offers some great activities and accommodation. Port Stanton is located on County Road 38.

historic steamboat

Swift Rapids: Lock #43

Swift Rapids lock is very secluded and quiet, hence its popularity with boaters who want a peaceful stop-over. The chamber holds 1.5 million gallons of water and takes approximately 6 minutes to fill. The sub-floor in the chamber has perforations to counter turbulence within the chamber. Boaters are reminded not to tie up to cleats. Once the chamber valve is opened, it can't be shut until the chamber is empty. If you tied to the cleat, you will be left high and dry, providing your cleats don't rip out.

Swift Rapids, Lock 43

Severn Falls
● ● ● ● ● ● ● ● ● ● ● ● ● ● ● ● ●

Severn Falls is a picturesque waterfront community downriver from Swift Rapids. The public wharf is right beside the marina and general store. There is plenty of accommodation within easy walking distance.

Big Chute: Marine Railway Lock #44

This picturesque area is famous for its marine railways which raise and lower boats 58 feet/17 m between the Severn River and Gloucester Pool. The original marine railway, built in 1917, is 26 feet/8 m long and is made of Douglas Fir. The second railway, constructed in 1977, is made of steel and can accommodate boats up to 100 feet/30.5 m in length. The platforms or "cars" travel up and down the railway tracks by means of huge winch cables which are powered by electric motors. Boats docked on the blue line are called to approach the carriage over a P.A. system. Boats must wait until they are called. During very busy operations, lock staff take names and numbers for orderly loading. The newer carriage can take boats 100 feet/35.6 m in length, provided the weight and draught do not exceed 90 tons/81.6 metric tonnes or 6 feet/2.15 m and the boat is not wider than 24 feet/8.5 m. Boats exceeding 75 tons/68 metric tonnes should contact Waterway Headquarters before entering the system (705)750-4900. The carriage itself weighs 110 tons and the crossing takes 7 minutes.

The boats are supported in the carriage by slings which must be individually placed to fit each boat. The staff members here stay fit by climbing all over the carriages, fitting slings every day. Boats sink into the slings in the water; they are not lifted. Slings must be placed at the ribs of the hull for proper support, so it helps if boats have sling markings on the side. Otherwise, the lock attendant must climb inside the boat to find reinforced areas. Although the staff here face a very demanding job, each boat is handled with extreme care.

There are 2 public wharves at Big Chute, one upriver and one downriver. The marina here has groceries, a snack bar and picnic facilities along with the usual marine services plus a great waterside restaurant and patio.

Big Chute Marine Railway

As you leave Big Chute, heading downriver, the channel becomes very winding and narrow. As a courtesy, boaters going upriver should give priority to downriver boaters as they are at a disadvantage due to the current.

The hydro generating station here, one of Ontario's first, opened in 1911. There is plenty to see around the railway here at Big Chute. Its diverse plantlife attracts a variety of species of wild life, and therefore makes it an interesting place to explore and make unusual discoveries. By road you will find Big Chute on County Roads 17 and 34.

Big Chute Marina

Navigation Note

Watch for cross currents below the Big Chute marine railways caused by the power generating station.

Big Chute Marine Railway, today

*Old Marine
Railway,
1975*

Port Severn: Lock #45

During May, spring run-off causes strong currents downstream from the lock. Weather warnings are given to boaters heading into Georgian Bay. These reports are based on radio reports and from the lockstaff's knowledge and first hand experience in the area.

Gloucester Pool is noted for excellent fishing, especially pickerel/walleye.

There are stores and restaurants within walking distance of the lock.

Chart no. 2029-2

MARINA	☾	H	⚡	⛽	⛽	⚓	🥤	⛵	⚓	🔧	🧒	🛏	🍴	🛒
❸ Big Chute Marina 705-756-2641	✓	✓	✓	✓		✓	✓	✓	✓	✓	✓	✓	✓	✓
❹ Severn Boat Haven 705-538-2975	✓	✓	✓	✓	✓	✓	✓		✓	✓	✓	✓	✓	✓
❺ J.C. Marine Services 705-538-0749	✓		✓			✓	✓	✓	✓	✓	✓	✓	✓	✓
❻ Driftwood Cove Resort 705-538-2502	✓		✓			✓	✓	✓			✓	✓		
❼ S R Boat Sales Ltd. 705-538-0500	✓	✓	✓	✓	✓	✓	✓	✓	✓	✓	✓			✓

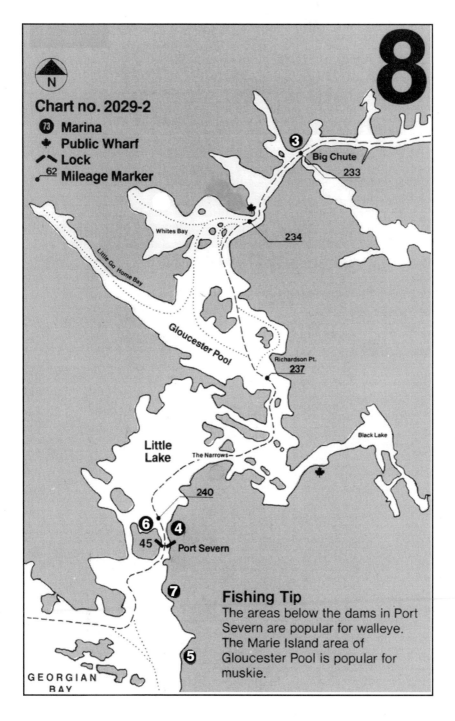

8

N

Chart no. 2029-2

73 **Marina**
✤ **Public Wharf**
⌃ **Lock**
•62 **Mileage Marker**

3 Big Chute
233

Whites Bay

Little Go Home Bay

234

Gloucester Pool

Richardson Pt.
237

Black Lake

Little Lake

The Narrows

240

6 **4**
45 **Port Severn**

7

GEORGIAN BAY

5

Fishing Tip
The areas below the dams in Port Severn are popular for walleye. The Marie Island area of Gloucester Pool is popular for muskie.

Port Severn

● ● ● ● ● ● ● ● ● ● ● ● ● ● ● ● ●

The Severn River flows into beautiful Georgian Bay, at Port Severn. Port Severn's lock 45 lowers the craft the final 14 feet/4.5 m out of the Trent-Severn Waterway.

This small community was once a thriving lumber town. Majestic white pine from the area were lumbered at Christie's Mill. The mill operated until 1896 when it was razed by fire after being struck by lightning. What remains of this time is the hotel, which was once the mill's boarding house, and a few log cabins.

Today, Port Severn has public docking, grocery stores, a post office, beer and liquor store, several marinas and great accommodation and dining.

This area boasts some of the finest muskie fishing in Canada during the late summer and fall, as well as good bass fishing in the summer and pickerel/walleye fishing in the spring. You will find Port Severn just off of Hwy 69.

Port Severn, Lock #45

Travel Notes

lock station at Severn Bridge

Area

Points North-Georgian Bay-North Channel-North of Superior

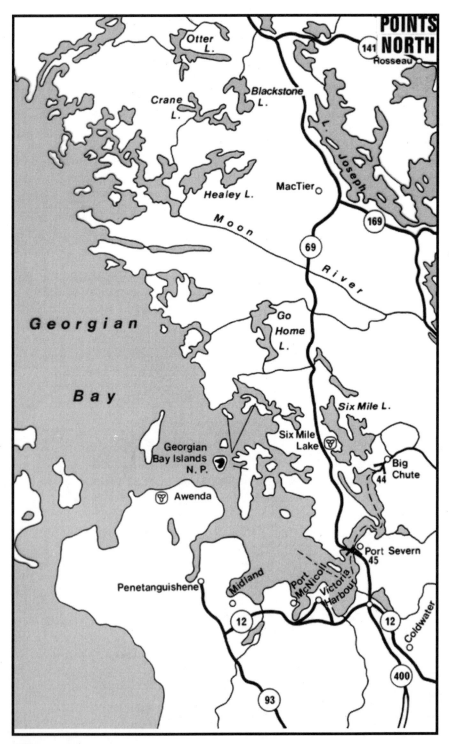

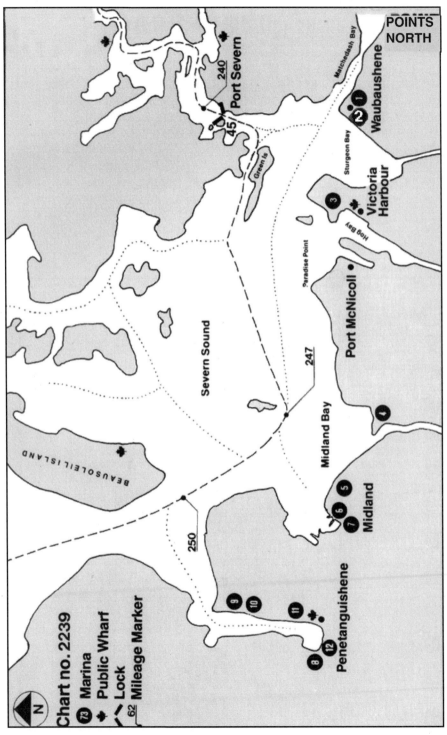

Waubaushene

● ● ● ● ● ● ● ● ● ● ● ● ● ● ●

The community of Waubaushene and Forest Harbour, linked by bridge, together have a population of approximately 2,400 year round residents. This number rises substantially with the influx of tourists and cottagers during the summer months. Located in Tay Township, Waubaushene might be called "the backdoor to Huronia" due to its proximity to such attractions as Wye Marsh and the Martyr's Shrine. This was a lumber town built around the success of the Georgian Bay Lumber Company.

There are a number of marinas and a government dock which is a short walk to nearby grocery stores. The library has public access to the internet and fax service should the need arise. There is a waterside park with a lovely beach, picnic and washroom facilities.

Chart no. 2239

MARINA	C☆	H	🔌	⛽	⛽	⚓	🚰	⚓	🛟	🔧	🚻	🛏	🍴	🛒
❶ Marsh's Marina 705-538-2285	✓		✓			✓	✓	✓	✓	✓	✓	✓		
❷ Nautical Masters Inc. 705-538-2461			✓				✓	✓	✓	✓	✓	✓		✓
❸ Queen's Cove Marina 705-534-4100	✓	✓	✓	✓	✓	✓	✓	✓	✓	✓	✓	✓	✓	✓
❹ Wye Heritage Marina 705-526-0155	✓		✓	✓	✓		✓	✓	✓	✓	✓	✓	✓	✓
❺ Midland Marina 705-526-4433	✓		✓	✓	✓	✓	✓	✓	✓	✓	✓	✓		
❻ Bay Port Yachting Cntr. 1-888-BAY PORT	✓		✓	✓	✓	✓	✓	✓	✓	✓	✓	✓	✻	✻
❼ Midland Harbour 705-526-4610	✓	✓	✓			✓					✓	✓	✓	✓
❽ Hindson Marine 705-549-2991	✓	✓	✓	✓	✓	✓	✓	✓	✓	✓	✓	✓	✓	✓
❾ Dutchman's Cove Marina 705-549-2641	✓		✓			✓	✓		✓	✓	✓	✓		
❿ Bay Moorings Yacht Club 705-549-6985	✓	✓	✓	✓	✓	✓	✓	✓	✓	✓	✓	✓	✓	✓
⓫ Harbour West Marina 705-549-9378	✓		✓	✓		✓	✓	✓	✓	✓	✓	✓		
⓬ Beacon Bayt Marina 705-549-2075	✓	✓	✓	✓	✓	✓	✓	✓	✓	✓	✓	✓	✻	✻

Victoria Harbour

●●●●●●●●●●●●●●●●●

This cottage area nestled in the crook of a sheltered bay on the south eastern shore of Georgian Bay was first settled by John Hogg who perhaps built one of the area's first sawmills. The settlement grew up around the mill.

Every summer thousands of tourists trek north to visit nearby historic sites. An atmosphere of home town charm awaits tourists who leave the highway to pass through Victoria Harbour. Behind its quiet facade lies a wealth of history. For boaters looking for provisions and other services Victoria Harbour is within walking distance of the marina. There is a liquor and beer store, post office, general store, cafes, grocery store, coin laundry, churches, pharmacy and medical centre. By car Victoria Harbour can be found on Hwy 69 and Hwy 400 from Barrie.

Honey Harbour

●●●●●●●●●●●●●●●●●●

The population of this village swells each summer with the influx of summer vacationers. Honey Harbour is a base for anglers, scuba divers, swimmers and campers who are attracted by nearby Beausoleil Island. A water taxi is available. In the main shopping district, there are restaurants, grocery stores, a church and a post office. You may be surprised to note that there is a dock at the liquor and beer store.

The Georgian Bay Islands National Park headquarters is in Honey Harbour and any information you should require regarding the park can be found there. To get to Honey Harbour by car you will have to take County Road 5 from Port Severn.

Midland

●●●●●●●●●●●●●●●●●●

Midland has a heritage reaching back to 1639, when Jesuit missionaries arrived from France to spread the word of God to the Huron natives. At the time, theirs was the only inland European settlement north of Mexico. Such an isolated existence would be hard to imagine if it weren't for the excellent reconstruction of the Sainte-Marie among the Hurons Mission. This palisaded settlement contains a hospital, blacksmith shop, workshop, a church and a longhouse. Guides are costumed in the garb of the period and demonstrate the operation of tools and implements used at the mission shops.

You can learn anything you want to know about marsh plant and animal life at the Wye Marsh Wildlife Centre. There are self-guiding nature trails and floating marsh boardwalks to assist visitors in this learning experience. The best way to reach the Wye Marsh is to follow the Wye River, past the Wye Heritage Marina until you come to public docks a few yards from the Centre. The Wye Marsh Wildlife Centre is just east of Sainte-Marie among the Hurons.

The Martyr's Shrine is also in this vicinity, just 50 yards or so across Highway 12. It was built in 1926 as a memorial to 6 of Canada's martyred Jesuit priests; among them was Father Brebeuf. Each year, many people make a pilgrimage to this magnificent Shrine.

On Little Lake Park, in town, there is the Huronia Museum with displays of Indian and Pioneer lifestyles and the Huron Indian Village, which is a replica of a 17th century Huron village.

Midland's present is as impressive as its past. The town dock is right at the foot of King Street. The city has a vast array of fine restaurants, clothing stores, grocery stores, craft shops, boutiques and cinemas for your choosing and a new waterfront park and trail.

In late June, Little Lake features the annual Bass Tournament and, on July 1st the Rotary Club hosts a gigantic barbecue at the town dock. The B.I.A. holds their annual sidewalk sale in mid-July. July also boasts the Open Fiddle and Stepdance Competition. Throughout July and August, the Midland Stage Company will be presenting a variety of productions for your enjoyment. Contact the Chamber of Commerce at (705) 526-7884 for more details.

If you'd like to leave the driving to someone else for 3 hours, you can relax on one of the 30,000 Island Cruises, which leaves from the town docks. Your tour guide will share a little of the local knowledge of the islands and bays with you. These bays and islands are a scuba diver's paradise. Compressed air for scuba tanks is available at the Fire Department, one block west of the town dock on the waterfront trail. Hwys 12 or 93 will take you into Midland.

KEY TO MIDLAND

1. Galerie Gale
2. Midland Civic Centre
3. Midland Curling Club
4. Midland Harbour Town Dock
5. Midland Centennial Arena
6. Y.M.C.A.
7. Midland Town Hall, Police Department
8. Royal Canadian Legion
9. Midland Town Centre (B.I.A.)
10. Ontario Provincial Police
11. Huronia District Hospital
12. Penetang- Midland Coach Lines
13. Post Office
14. The Beer Store (2 Loc.)
15. Midland Public Library
16. LCBO
17. Budd Watson Gallery
18. Castle Village Gift Shops & Dracula's Dungeon
19. Martyr's Shrine
20. Sainte-Marie among the Hurons
21. Wye Marsh Wildlife Centre
22. Huron Indian Village
23. Huronia Museum
24. Miss Midland Cruises
25. Lawn Bowling & Shuffleboard
26. Brooklea Golf & Country Club
27. Midland Golf & Country Club
28. Roxy Theatre
29. Midland Drive-In
30. Smith's Mobile Homes & Trailer Park
31. Park Villa Motel
32. Shamrock Motel
33. Panorama Motel
34. Chalet Motel
35. Midway Motel
36. Highland Inn & Convention Centre
37. Mountainview Mall
38. Huronia Mall
39. Downtown Midland
40. Comfort Inn

Enjoy Our Parks

A. **McCullough Park**:
~swimming

B. Peter Peterson Park:
~swimming
~washrooms/changerooms
~boat launching ramp
~picnic area

C. **Woodland Park**
~ball diamond
~playground

D. **Huronia Park**
~picnic area
~playground

E. **Little Lake Park**
~picnic areas
~tennis courts
~camping
~swimming
~changerooms/washrooms
~food concession
~mini-golf
~pedal boats
~lawnbowling & Shuffleboard

F. **Herb Beauchamp Memorial Athletic Field** ~ball diamond

G. Sainte-Marie Park
~picnic areas
~barbeques
~shelters
~washrooms
~boat cruises

H. **Tiffin Park**
~tennis courts
~ball diamond
~picnic area
~scenic lookout

I. **Bayview Park**
~play area/ball diamond

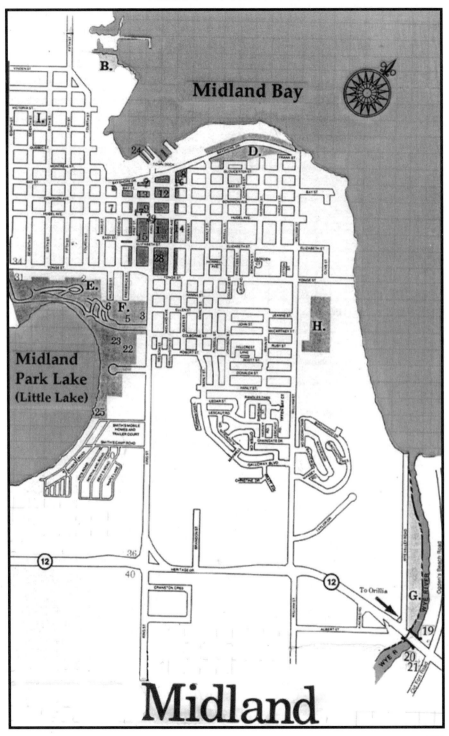

Midland Bay

Midland
Park Lake
(Little Lake)

To Orillia

Midland

Sainte-Marie

●●●●●●●●●●●●●●●●

This internationally significant historic attraction is on Highway 12, east of Midland, opposite Martyrs' Shrine. Established in 1639, Sainte-Marie was the headquarters of the French Jesuit mission to the Hurons and was the first European community in Ontario.

Abandoned and burned by the French in 1649, Sainte-Marie now stands recreated on the original site of the banks of the Wye River. Today's visitors enjoy an introductory audio-visual show, and then enter the historic area where they explore more than a dozen Native and European structures. 17th century-style stables house cows, chickens and pigs. Site maps make touring easy and costumed historical interpreters answer questions and point out highlights.

The Sainte-Marie museum is an adventure in discovery which leads visitors through 17th-century French and Native Huron artifacts and displays.

During the summer months, visitors may participate in one of their daily 'hands-on' presentations learning 17th-century fire-starting techniques, listening to legends in the Longhouse or they can enjoy canoe excursions, lasting 90 minutes, paddling in 26' canoes down the Wye River with qualified instructors.

canoe excursion at Sainte-Marie among the Hurons

Daily, visitors may enjoy browsing in the Museum Gift Shop or just relaxing in the air-conditioned comfort of the Restaurant that is fully licensed and offers a barbeque outdoors, snacks and light meals throughout the day. Sunday evenings during July and August enjoy listening to live Jazz Bands and All-you-can-eat BBQ Buffet.

Sainte-Marie among the Hurons is open every day from Victoria Day Weekend until Canadian Thanksgiving from 10:00 a.m. to 5:00 p.m. and offers a variety of educational tours. For further information please call (705) 526-7838.

Discovery Harbour in Historic Penetanguishene
•••••••••••••••••

Set your sails for adventure at Discovery Harbour!

Discovery Harbour, originally the site of a 19th-century British naval outpost, is now a picturesque marine heritage site located on the shoreline of Penetanguishene Bay. Over the past few years this popular site has seen much development and now offers many activities for a great family day outing.

Upon entering, visitors can stroll the beautiful waterside boardwalk as they approach the main entrance to the site. Of special note to boaters, the site now has **new visitor docks** located between Magazine Island an the shore line with an approximate depth of 5'. In view are the impressive replica sailing ships H.M..S. *Tecumseth* and H.M.S. *Bee*. Along the shoreline are the Historic Properties which can be toured for a fascinating glimpse into 19th century life. Children can try out a sailor's hammock, experience what it was like to be a dock-yard shipwright, and even go on-board the *Tecumseth* or *Bee* to inspect the miles of rigging or ring the ships bell. Also on the property is the original 1845 Officers' Quarters, a magnificent example of a lavishly furnished Georgian residence which is a real hit with antique and history buffs.

For those with a taste for adventure, Discovery Harbour also offers unique historic sailing programs in the summertime. Visitors can go out aboard the *Tecumseth* or *Bee* for an afternoon , evening or a full day "hands on" sail and help the enthusiastic crew handle these magnificent ships in the same manner as they were sailed in olden times.

The King's Wharf Theatre, located on site, offers a selection of diverse entertainment year-round. Also on location is Discovery Harbour's waterside restaurant, *Captain Roberts' Table.*

Discovery Harbour is open late May through Labour Day in early September. Call (705) 549-8064 for admission details or for sailing program information. You can also visit their internet site at http://www.on.ca/discover/

Historic sailing program at Discovery Harbour

Penetanguishene

●●●●●●●●●●●●●●●●●●

B ienvenue and welcome to Penetanguishene... 'the Gateway to
the 30,000 Islands'. This unique community of 7,000 boasts a
rich heritage of being one of the first settled communities in Ontario.
Many French voyageurs settled this area around the original 19th century Naval and Military Base, known today as Discovery Harbour. As
you enter town you will notice the twin angels symbolizing the goodwill between French and English.

Experience the friendliness of this town as you make your way
down Main Street visiting fine boutiques and restaurants.

If getting out on the water is your pleasure, Penetanguishene has a
choice of cruises second to none.

There are boat charter operators ready to cater to your every whim.
You can explore shipwrecks at the bottom of the harbour, picnic on an
island, go fishing with an experienced guide, or just soak up the beauty of the region. Take an afternoon cruise aboard the *Georgian Queen*
or one of their scheduled evening jazz cruises. If sail training is a
dream of yours, you can make it a reality by spending the day, afternoon or evening aboard the historic ships *Bee* or *Tecumseth*. Finally if
you want the ultimate in luxury cruises, book a 3, 4 or 7 day excursion
on the brand new Georgian Clipper, a memorable vacation that will
last a lifetime.

Centennial Museum, built around 1870 as a commercial building,
now houses many artifacts of the late 19th and early 20th centuries.
Extensive renovations and additions to the site will give visitors a
clear picture of yesteryear. Join in one of the Sunday evening outdoor
concerts featuring local artists performing by the bay.

The Penetanguishene-Tiny Chamber of Commerce invites everyone
to join them for their annual special events. A kick off to summer
starts with the Georgian Bay Heritage Festival in mid-June. A cultural
celebration of their diverse region, featuring Pow Wows, tall ship
tours, a Victorian Tea, log sawing demonstrations, old fashioned
games to name a few of the activities. Join them for Canada Day, a
weekend filled with activities. The Georgian Bay Poker Run, called
the "Grand Daddy" of poker runs, will be held for the fourth time in
Penetanguishene on the long weekend in August, 1997. A spectacular
event for participants and spectators alike. Watch as some of the

world's fastest boats compete.

Winter is also a time of great recreational activities. Extensive snowmobile trails allow visitors miles and miles of sledding on groomed trails. Several ski resorts offer both nordic and alpine skiing. Don't forget about ice fishing. Penetanguishene is proud to host the 50th annual Winterama in February 1998, the oldest running winter carnival in Ontario.

There is plenty of accommodation in Penetanguishene from B&Bs to hotels to campgrounds. Contact the Penetanguishene-Tiny Chamber of Commerce for more information at 705-549-2232 or visit their website:www.huronet.com/chamb_commerce

peace and tranquility on Georgian Bay

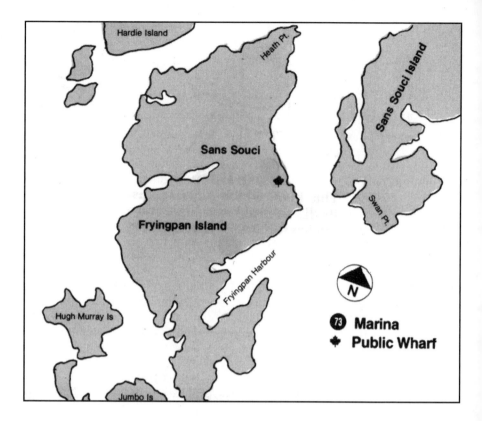

The map shows labels: Hardie Island, Heath Pt., Sans Souci Island, Sans Souci, Swan Pt., Fryingpan Island, Fryingpan Harbour, Hugh Murray Is, Jumbo Is, N, **73 Marina**, **Public Wharf**

Sans Souci

● ● ● ● ● ● ● ● ● ● ● ● ● ● ● ●

This small summer community is located on Frying Pan Island, about 16 miles/26 kms south of Parry Sound. Because it is right on the small craft channel, boaters en route to ports north and south make a point of stopping at Sans Souci's well-protected, deep water harbour. Bass and pickerel/walleye seem to like this area as much as boaters do; fishing here is excellent. Apart from the island's natural beauty, good fishing and hiking trails, you'll find everything you might need. There is a post office, grocery store, general store, restaurants and marinas with day and overnight docking.

San Souci is more than just a haven in Georgian Bay. It is a charming and picturesque community that is well worth a visit. Motorists can get to Sans Souci via water taxi from Honey Harbour.

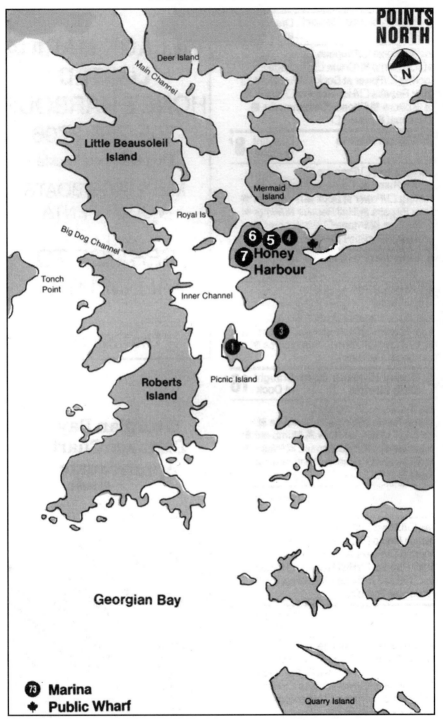

Chart no. Georgian Bay

MARINA	☪	H	⚡	🛥	⛽	🪫	⚓	🚰	🛗	📷	🔧	🚻	🛏	🍽	🛒
1 Picnic Island Marina 705-756-2421			✓	✓	✓	✓	✓				✓			✓	✓
3 Paragon Marina 705-756-2402	✓		✓	✓		✓	✓	✓	✓	✓	✓	✓			
4 Honey Harbour Boat Club 705-756-2411	✓		✓	✓		✓		✓	✓	✓	✓				
5 Admiral's Marina 705-756-2432	✓		✓	✓	✓	✓	✓	✓		✓	✓	✓	✓		
6 Bayview Marina 705-756-2482	✓		✓	✓		✓	✓	✓	✓	✓	✓	✓			
7 South Bay Cove 705-756-3333	✓	✓	✓	✓	✓	✓	✓	✓	✓	✓	✓	✓	✓	✓	✓

Georgian Bay Islands National Park- Docking

Georgian Bay Islands National Park- Camping

Georgian Bay Islands
National Park

●●●●●●●●●●●●●●●●●●

South eastern Georgian Bay is spectacular for its windswept pines, glacier scraped rock, ancient forests and lush wetlands. The edge of the Canadian Shield meeting limestone bedrock and the glacial deposits of Southern Ontario make this corner of Georgian Bay a particularly attractive destination. Georgian Bay Islands National Park is a spectacular example of the 30,000 Islands ecosystem. These magnificent islands are outstanding for the diversity of habitats and species they support. The natural character and beauty attract thousands of visitors to its campsites, trails and docks every year.

This 59 island park stretches along the eastern shoreline of Georgian Bay from Twelve Mile Bay to as far south as the Severn Sound area. Beausoleil Island, largest of the park islands, is ideal for anchoring or docking overnight. If your itinerary includes more than one night stay, you can moor in protected coves and bays or camp at any one of 15 campgrounds. Campgrounds and docks vary in size and all have an adjacent trail to the main walking trails. Visitors can reserve campsites at the Cedar Spring campground by telephoning (705) 756-5909 after May 1st until Labour Day.

Most park facilities are about a 15 minute boat ride from Honey Harbour at the end of Muskoka Road 5, off Hwy 69 at Port Severn. Heritage Education programs are offered during the summer. Be sure to enquire about the park's access dock and camping sites located at Cedar Spring.

For further information contact: Georgian Bay Islands National Park, P.O. Box 28, Honey Harbour, Ontario, P0E 1E0. Telephone: (705) 756-2415

Basking at Georgian Bay Islands National Park

The North Channel &
North of Superior

● ● ● ● ● ● ● ● ● ● ● ● ● ● ● ●

In addition to Georgian Bay Islands National Park, Parks Canada also operates Bruce Peninsula National Park and Fathom Five National Marine Park, Canada's first national marine park off the northern tip of "the Bruce". Tobermory, at the end of Highway 6, is the jumping off point for land based visitors to access the 19 park islands included in Fathom Five. Whether arriving by private boat or taking one of the tour boats, this is an area of intrigue and rugged beauty. There are the remains of 21 known sail and steam ships, dating back to the mid-19th century, scattered about the bottom of Fathom Five. Records show others missing in this region and still uncharted. These wrecks provide divers and sightseers with a great historic viewing opportunity.

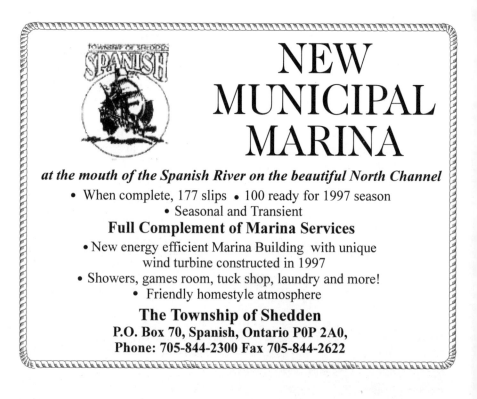

The great waters of Georgian Bay provide access to the spectacular cruising grounds offered by the neighbouring North Channel sheltered from Lake Huron by Manitoulin Island and others leading all the way from Kilarney to Sault Ste. Marie some 160 miles/250 kms to the west. The North Channel Marine Tourism Council is working hard to acquaint boaters of all types about the host of cruising opportunities available in this region. Boaters interested in this region can write or call for a complete information kit that includes an excellent brochure, marina listings and informative video. Work is already underway on a CD Rom of the North Channel route.

The North Channel is a region of contrasts and extremes as the literature states. While the area features a vast number of uninhabited islands by contrast the stretch of water through Sault Ste. Marie is the busiest waterway in the world. Here can be found complete solitude yet within close distances any required amenity or service can be found.

The "Soo", a city of some 80,000 residents, marks the gateway to the North of Superior cruising region. The vast coastline of Lake Superior's north shore stretches more than 400 miles/644 kms between Sault Ste. Marie and Thunder Bay further west. This area offers everything from sand beaches to towering bluffs that plunge into the sparkling waters of the world's largest fresh water sea. Here can be found isolated anchorages or the comforts of full service mari-

Rossport, Superior's north shore

nas and great northern hospitality in the small towns and villages that hug the north shore. Lake Superior's waters offer excellent fishing for lake trout, rainbows, salmon and white fish. The Roberta Bondar Marina in the heart of the "Soo" is the perfect stop over or launch point for a really unique coastal cruising experience. The Sault Locks on the Canadian side of the seaway closed for many years due to wall decay are now undergoing a multi million dollar rehabilitation and are scheduled to re-open to boating traffic in the summer of 1997.

Wildlife at Pukaskwa National Park

Many of the communities along the Trans Canada Highway 17 route west that skirts the North Superior shore offer good boating access points for those trailering vessels or wanting to rent boats and explore this area by section each year. The vacation opportunities are endless. Many of the anchorages to be found were favourite stopovers for the voyageurs of the fur trade era. Pukaskwa National Park is a hot spot for canoeists and sea kayakers. Visitors to this park will agree with the Parks Canada brochure that calls Pukaskwa wild, awesome and fascinating. A coastal hiking trail winds through Canadian Shield country forests for more than 37 miles/58 kms from Hattie Cove, the centre for most park activity, services and anchorage to the North Swallow River.

aerial view, North of Superior

The community of Wawa before Pukaskwa and Marathon, Terrace Bay, Rossport, Nipigon, Red Rock and Thunder Bay further on all offer visiting boaters good marina facilities and provisioning services. The North of Superior Marina Marketing Association like its counterparts for the North Channel and the Trent-Severn offer visitors a comprehensive information package to assist with vacation and cruise planning. In addition to a colourful brochure and video, the marketing association can also provide those interested with a marina guide covering north shore of Superior services from Sault Ste. Marie to beyond Thunder Bay. The association is also working to identify a number of "safe" harbours along the route where boaters between communities can tuck in during inclement weather which will work effectively to further popularize this cruising route.

Planning an extraordinary waterway adventure to the North Channel or the North of Superior requires some time and careful preparation so be sure to use the services provided in this waterway guide to help ensure a safe and fun filled cruising vacation.
Contact:
The North Channel Marine Tourism Council, PO Box 70, Spanish, Ontario, POP 2AO, 1-800-563-8719.

North of Superior Tourism Association, 1119 Victoria Avenue East, Thunder Bay, Ontario, P7C 1B7, 1-800-265-3951.

North of Superior Landscape

Fishing
Guide

Fishing
Guide

Fishing Guide

• • • • • • • • • • • • • • • • • •

Introduction

Fishing is the perfect boating activity because you can do it with the whole family or you can do it alone when you need some peace and quiet.

As with most boating activities, there are a few important things to keep in mind. For example, a good angler should show respect for private property, public waterways and the rights of other anglers. One way of showing this respect is to leave the environment as clean as it was before you got there.

Another thing to keep in mind is the need to put safety first in the use of fishing equipment and in your enjoyment of the sport. Anglers with some experience should always share their safety knowledge with those who are just learning to fish.

As well as sharing safety, there is a tradition among anglers of sharing their skills with beginners. Many a young person has become an enthusiastic angler because someone took the time to share his or her experience.

Beginners need to know about the importance of fishing regulations, how to avoid damaging the natural habitat, and last but not least, beginners need to learn respect for fish in general, before and after catching them.

Trent-Severn Highlights

●●●●●●●●●●●●●●●●●●●

Some of the best warm water fishing in southern Ontario is found in the Kawartha Lakes. This region is renowned for yellow pickerel/walleye, muskellunge, smallmouth and largemouth bass. In addition, the Kawarthas support large populations of panfish such as rock bass, yellow perch, sunfish and bullheads.

Lake Simcoe is a favourite with anglers throughout the year. During the spring, lake trout, northern pike, yellow perch and whitefish are readily available. In the summer, smallmouth and largemouth bass, lake trout, whitefish and occasionally muskellunge are popular.

Trophy muskellunge, northern pike and yellow pickerel are caught in Georgian Bay every year. The best times for fishing pickerel and northerns in Georgian Bay are May and June, and September, October and November. Smallmouth bass and yellow perch also abound in Georgian Bay. The bass bite better during July and August. But be prepared as the water of Georgian Bay can be rough.

Coho salmon were recently introduced into Lake Ontario and provide exciting angling in the lake and in some of the rivers east of Toronto. In fact, many of the streams and rivers running into Lake Ontario feature spring and fall runs of rainbow trout and coho salmon.

Big Fish!

There are many rules and regulations to keep in mind, ask the Ministry of Natural Resources for a copy of the Ontario Sport Fishing Regulations Summary.

For information on fishing rules and regulations, licenses and special events for anglers contact one of the following organizations:

Ontario Ministry of Natural Resources   (705) 755-2551

Ontario Federation of Anglers and Hunters   (705) 748-6324

Ontario's Conservation Authorities   (705) 745-5791

Northern Ontario Tourist Outfitters   (705) 472-5552

Resorts Ontario   (705) 325-9115

Ontario Family Fishing Weekend Event Information Line
       1-800-667-1940

For additional information write, phone or visit the Ministry of Natural Resources:

Ministry of Natural Resources
300 Water Street, P.O. Box 7000,
Peterborough, ON, K9J 8M5
General Inquiry -   (705) 755-2000

Natural Resources Information Centre
in Toronto   (416) 314-2000
French Inquiry   (416) 314-1665

pickerel /walleye

Waterway Wildlife

Great Blue Heron

Perhaps one of the most majestic sights on the waterway is this great long-legged bird. As it glides along the river air currents, its large feet drag out behind like an airborne rudder.

Great Blue Herons, which migrate in the fall, return to this area by early April and start nesting in colonies. The male lays the framework of branches and twigs across the branch of a tree. The female lines the nest with leaves and moss, where she will eventually lay three to five bluish-green eggs. Within the heron colonies, there may be as many as ten nests in one tree. If the young chicks are disturbed by predators or curious humans, they become highly agitated and often bump each other out of the nest with fatal results. Those that survive will grow to over 3 feet in length at maturity.

Herons are wading birds and are often seen in marshy areas during the day hunting for frogs and snakes or fishing the river at night for minnows and sunfish. When they stand perfectly still on a riverside rock, they are often mistaken for a dead tree branch.

Waterway Wildlife

● ● ● ● ● ● ● ● ● ● ● ● ● ● ● ● ●

Gulls and Terns

Although closely related, gulls tend to be larger than terns, especially Herring gulls. Herring gulls are about two feet long and are white, except for their grey and black wings and back. Their bills are yellow and somewhat hooked. The young are brownish grey and speckled until maturity at three years. Their legs are fairly long and their feet are webbed.

Terns are smaller, being about fifteen inches long. Common terns have white bodies, black-capped heads and grey backs and wings. Their bills are red with black tips. On the whole, they are more streamlined birds with much more slender wings.

Both species are graceful flyers and seem to enjoy climbing to great heights just for the fun of soaring and gliding. Of course, part of the frolic entails keeping a sharp lookout for fish and floating debris to eat. Terns are better divers than gulls and fish is their main diet. Herring gulls are scavengers and will eat just about anything. They are often found in farmers' fields eating leftovers from harvest or picking away at garbage dumps. Whereas terns usually always nest in colonies, herring gulls may or may not. Sometimes they prefer to nest alone. Both species make their nests in shallow hollows on the ground which they surround with grasses and sticks. The females lay one to four eggs. Herring gull eggs are a mottled olive colour with brown and grey markings. Common tern eggs are smaller and mottled buff coloured with brown and greenish-grey markings. The parents regurgitate food to feed the chicks until they are old enough to feed themselves.

Waterway Wildlife

●●●●●●●●●●●●●●●●●

Belted Kingfisher

At first glance, you may think this flash of blue and white is a blue jay, but a closer look will reveal orangey-brown markings on its breast and a tuft of unruly head plumage. Kingfishers are true to their name: reigning supreme in the art of fast, productive fishing. They will perch on a branch overlooking the river until a fish is sighted, and in the blink of an eye, will dart out and dive into the water, catching the fish between their jaws. Kingfishers then take their catch back to the perch where they knock it senseless before eating it.

Kingfishers nest in burrows along the river bank. The female lays five to eight pinkish-white eggs and both parents incubate until the chicks are hatched. Many young kingfishers drown while trying to master their parents' fishing abilities.

Waterway Wildlife

Loons

Some quiet night or misty morning, you may hear the haunting lament of the common loon. Loons are diving birds that have long, streamlined bodies and large webbed feet which are found at the very tail-end of their bodies. It is this placement of the legs that makes loons look so ungainly on land where they lay their eggs. The nests are built at the shoreline and generally only one pair of loons will nest in the given area. There are no loon colonies. The female lays two eggs which are khaki-coloured with black spots. Providing that the nest is not swamped by the wake of speedboats, the chicks hatch after a month. Once hatched, the chicks acclimatize themselves to their new surroundings for a day or two and then head for the water. It is another two months before they will be able to fly.

Loons eat fish for which they dive. They have been known to dive to depths of thirty feet. They can also swim underwater for up to two minutes without emerging for air. They fly well too, once they are actually airborne. While trying to get airborne, they look like characters from cartoons as they run and flap their way across the water. Their landings, as well, are fairly clumsy. They seem to crash into the water with no control.

The number of these beautiful birds is decreasing. If you spot a pair or a family, enjoy them from afar so they won't be frightened.

Friends of the Trent-Severn Waterway

Who are they?

A group of enthusiastic and dedicated volunteers working in co-operation with the staff of the Trent-Severn Waterway to protect and interpret the waterway's natural, historical and recreational resources.

What do they do?

- Welcome visitors to our Safe and Friendly Waterway
- Operate Sales and Information Outlets
- Encourage greater co-operation between Waterway communities
- Promote goodwill and understanding with similiar organizations within Canada and abroad.

If you become a member you receive...

- **AHOY!** Our quarterly newsletter
- Boat Cruises and Special events
- 10% discount on purchases of books and souveniers (in person or by mail).

----**Yes, I wish to support the activities of the FTSW!**
☐Please send me a mail-order catalogue
☐Here is my application for membership

Name _____

Address _____

Postal Code _____   ☐ $20.00 Family

Telephone #:_____   ☐ $50.00 Corporate

Make cheque payable to: **Friends of Trent Severn Waterway**
and send to: FTSW, Box 572, Peterborough, Ontario, K9J 6Z6
1-800-663-2628

General Informaton

• • • • • • • • • • • • • • • • • •

Hours of Operation for 1997

TRENT-SEVERN WATERWAY

Box 567, Peterborough, Ontario, K9J 6Z6
(705)750-4900

May 16 - June 19	Monday to Thursday	10:00am to 4:00pm
	Friday to Sunday	9:00am to 7:30pm
	Holiday Monday	9:00am to 7:30pm
June 20 - August 10		8:30am to 8:30pm
August 11 - Sept. 1		8:30am to 7:30pm
Sept. 2 - Oct. 15	Monday to Friday	10:00am to 4:00pm
	Saturday and Sunday	9:00am to 6:00pm
	Thanksgiving Monday	9:00am to 6:00pm

*Note last lockage at most lockstations occurs half an hour prior to station closure.
**Last Bridge Swing occurs ten minutes prior to station closure
(**Please Note**: The hours above are for 1997 only, they are subject to change. We recommend phoning to confirm hours and rates before departure.)

1997 Permits and Fees for Lockage and Mooring

Single Lockage and Return:	$0.55/ft.	($1.80/m)
One Day:	$1.25/ft.	($4.10/m)
Six Day:	$4.00/ft.	($13.12/m)
Seasonal Lockage	$7.00/ft)	($22.96/m)
Transit:	$3.65/ft.	($11.97/m)
Overnight Mooring:	$0.45/ft.	($1.48/m)
Seasonal Overnight Mooring	$6.70/ft.	($22.00/m)

* A minimum 12 ft vessel length fee will be instituted for vessels under 12 ft.

Overnight Camping fees

Group:	$10.00 per party up to 10 persons
Individual:	$10.00 min. and $1.50/each additional

Big Chute Marine Railways

When both marine railways are in operation, vessel operators must adhere to the boat marshalling instructions.

New Marine Railway: The maximum size of vessel which will be carried on the new marine railway is:

Displacement........90t		Beam ....7.3m(24ft.)	
Length ....30.4 m(100ft)		Draught...........1.8m(6ft.)	

Operators whose vessels have a peculiar hull configuration or who forsee problems in lifting the hull by sling or whose weight exceeds 75tons or 68 metric tonnes should contact the Superintendent of the Trent-Severn Waterway.

Old Marine Railway: The old marine railway will be operated when required by the vilume of traffic.

Displacement........18t		Beam ....4m(13ft.)	
Length ....15.2m(50ft.)		Draught...........1.2m(4ft.)	

Little Chute, km 380.5 (mile 236.4)to km380.75 (mile 236.6) Strong currents exist through this narrow section of the waterway. Boat operators are advised to use caution when entering the Narrows or approaching on-coming traffic.

Lockchamber Fire Safety Signs

Turn engine off — No open flames — No smoking — Leave bilge blower on

Approaching a Lock

The "Blue Line" is a painted blue strip on the concrete walls above and below each lock. By tying your boat up at the Blue Line you indicate to the lock staff that you wish passage through. Three toots of your horn will also alert lock and bridge staff to your intentions.

Remain securely tied up until the lock staff instruct you otherwise. At some locks, a green traffic light will be your signal to proceed into the lock chamber.

Entering the Lock

Move off the Blue Line in order as indicated by lock staff.

Houseboats are particularly susceptible to the whims of the wind, so be aware of wind speed and direction, and listen to the advice of lock staff as you enter the lock.

Your crew (adults, if possible) should be posted at bow and stern and have their lines nearby, neatly coiled and free of knots. Concentrate on coming in straight, using the reverse gear of your motor to slow down.

As you near the black holding cables attached to the walls of the lock chamber, have your crew members ready to loop their lines around the cables. On busy days, it may be necessary to loop your lines to a neighbouring boat.

Be alert to other boats entering behind you and move forward if necessary. **Do not fend a moving boat off a wall with your hands or feet.** It can lead to serious injury. Use a boat hook.

Once safely positioned inside the lock chamber, **turn off your engine and do not smoke or use open-flame appliances.** Never leave your boat unattended in the lock.

Be prepared to show your permit to lock staff or be ready to purchase one from them.

General Notes

-For safety reasons, vessel operators and passengers should not smoke, idle engines or operate open flame appliances during a lock operation or restart engines until directed by lock operators.

-Vessels are prohibited under Canal Regulations from mooring on blue line areas during operating hours except while waiting for lockage.

-Vessel operators may obtain a permit from the Lockmaster to use canal grounds for camping up to a maximum of 48 hours per lock station. Camping in any other areas or with self-contained motor vehicles on Canal property is prohibited.

-Times given are local time.

-No vessels shall be moored to a canal wharf or wall for a period in excess of 48 hours. Vessels having reached this maximum length of stay shall not return to the wharf or wall for 24 hours.

-Docking fees, based on the vessel length, will be levied at some canals.

-Vessel operators and visitors are advised to exercise extreme caution in the vicinity of dams because of dangerous current and undertows.

-Watch your wake. Vessel operators are requested to operate their vessels in a manner which will reduce wake action in narrow channels. Remember that breaking waves erode banks.

-Vessel operators using the canals should read "Boating Safely" which is available from lockstations.

Conversion Chart

Kilometres x .6214 = Miles
Litres x .2642 = U.S. Gallons
Metres x 3.2808 = Feet
Kilograms x 2.2046 = Pounds
(Celsius x 1.8) + 32 = Fahrenheit

Navigation Notes

There are 3 areas in particular where boaters are advised to take extra precaution.

1. Canal and Mitchell Lakes
These lakes can be treacherous because of stumps and logs which sometimes float into the channel.

2. Lakes Simcoe and Couchiching
Storms can blow up quite suddenly on these lakes and boaters should ask about weather conditions at locks 41 and 42 and at marinas in the vicinity of the Atherley Narrows before entering the lakes.

3. Big Chute
The winding channel below Big Chute marine railways has a very strong cross current. If you are not familiar with these waters ask the operators of the marine railways for instructions.

Speed Limits

Boaters are cautioned that certain sections of the Waterway have speed limits. These sections are usually narrow channels or canal cuts, congested traffic areas and difficult navigation channels.

There are two types of signs- the boundary marker, which marks the beginning or end of a speed limit section, and the speed limit sign, which acts as a reminder.

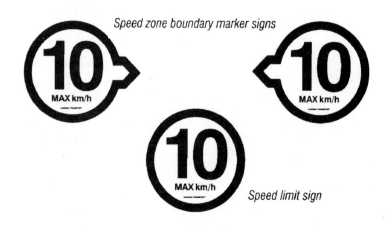

Speed zone boundary marker signs

Speed limit sign

Draught

The navigation draught, as defined in the Canadian Nautical Charts for the Trent-Severn Waterway, is the controlled water depth over the lock sills. The Waterway between Lock #1 Trenton Lock and Lock #19 Scott's Mills Lock has a water depth over the sills of 2.44 metres (8 feet) and a water depth of 1.93 metres (6 feet) between Lock #19 Scott's Mills Lock and Lock #45 Port Severn. Any vessel drawing more than 5 feet/1.52 metres must contact the Trent-Severn Waterway office in Peterborough. (705) 750-4900.

Overhead Clearances

The minimum charted clearance for the Trent/Severn Waterway is 22 feet/6.7 m. On occasion and usually before navigation season exceptionally high water levels will reduce the actual clearance at the bridge at mile 87.34 to 15 feet/4.5 m.

The minimum charted overhead clearance in the Scugog area of the Waterway is 3m (10 feet) at a bridge at Lindsay. High water levels may reduce this to 2.5m (8.5 feet).

For specific clearances refer to the detailed Hydrographic Charts.

Customs

Boats entering Canada from foreign ports are required to obtain clearance papers from the Collector of Customs at a Port of Entry.

For boats approaching the Waterway from Lake Ontario, you must phone the customs office from Trenton.The office is located in Belleville. For boats approaching the Waterway from Georgian Bay there is a customs office at Midland.

Ports of Entry on the Trent-Severn Waterway are located at Orillia, Peterborough, Lindsay and Barrie.

For further information write to: Revenue Canada, Dominion Public Building, 1 Front St. W., Station A, Toronto, Ontario M5W 1A3 or call 1-800-461-9999.

Policing the Waterway
●●●●●●●●●●●●●●●●●●●

Boating and enjoying the waterway should be a fun filled experience. And to help ensure it stays that way, waterway visitors cruising the system, chartering a houseboat or travelling in smaller vessels are reminded to exercise care and common sense at all times. This applies to the proper handling of boats, keeping wakes to a minimum, consumption of alcohol and being environmentally sensitive.

For those living and doing business along the waterway, water quality is very important. Don't litter! Keep waste products aboard for safe and clean removal at appropriate marinas and docks and keep noise levels to a minimum. Sound really carries over the water. All these obvious tips are enshrined in laws that are firmly enforced by a number of police services that patrol the Trent-Severn during the summer months to take care of those who choose to ignore the "rules of the road."

The Ontario Provincial Police have a number of marine patrols that cover the waterway. Under a new ticketing system officers can issue on the spot citations for a variety of boating infractions. The fines are fairly tough. For example: insufficient number of lifejackets or personal flotation devices, $205; insufficient oars, paddles or anchor, $155; missing bailer or manual pump, $205; prescribed fire extinguisher missing, $205; speeding $120; mooring in a navigation channel, $185.

Also, remember boaters acting in an irresponsible manner can also be denied passage through a lock. Alcohol and boating don't mix. A reminder too that it is illegal to operate or have care and control of a vessel whether it is in motion or not while one's ability to do so is impaired by alcohol or drugs or while one's alcohol blood level is over 80 milligrams per 100 milligrams of blood. Police officers have the authority to demand breath samples from vessel operators where alcohol consumption is reasonably suspected.

In addition to minimum fines of $300 upon conviction, a guilty person will be prohibited from operating a vessel for a minimum of three months and possibly up to three years. Liquor may be carried and consumed aboard pleasure boats under certain conditions. The boats must qualify as a private place in that they must have permanent sleeping accommodations, permanent cooking facilities and sanitary facilities. Furthermore it must be at anchor or secured to a dock or land to qualify. While underway a boat is subject to special rules. Any onboard liquor must be in an unopened container and seal unbroken or in a closed compartment. No one onboard is allowed to drink while a boat is underway. Police have the authority to enter and search a boat and its occupants where there are reasonable grounds to believe liquor is unlawfully kept. This can result in charges and confiscation of liquor products due to improper storage.

The OPP have a province-wide toll free telephone number 1-888-310-1122. It can also be accessed by cellular phone (Bell or Cantel) by dialing *OPP or *677.

locking through with OPP

Visitor Information Services
● ● ● ● ● ● ● ● ● ● ● ● ● ● ● ● ● ● ●

It is important to preplan your visit to the Trent-Severn Waterway. The following groups are available to lend a helping hand:

Ontario Travel
Toll Free in North America 1-800-ONTARIO (668-2746)
For Toronto area   English (416)314-0944
                      French (416)314-0956
                      TTY   (416) 314-6557

Parks Canada~Trent-Severn Waterway Headquarters
Box 567, Peterborough, On K9J 6Z6 (705)750-4900

Friends of the Trent-Severn Waterway
P.O. Box 572, Peterborough, On K9J 6Z6 (705)742-2251 Fax: (705)750-4816
email: FTSW@PTBO.IGS.NET   website:www.ptbo.igs.net/~ftsw

FTSW - CRUISE PLANNING ASSISTANCE: 1-800-663-2628

Ontario Marina Operators Association
4 Cataraqui St. Suite 211, Kingston, On, K7K 1Z7 (613) 547-6662 Fax:(613)547-6813 email:omoa@marinasontario.com website:www.marinasontario.com

Cobourg Tourist Information Centre
212 King St. W. Cobourg, On (905) 372-5831 1-888-Cobourg
Fax: (905) 372-2411 email: cobourg-cofc@eagle.ca

Belleville Chamber of Commerce
Box 726 Belleville, On K8N 5B3 (613) 962-4597 Fax: (613) 962-3911
email: chamber@city.belleville.on.ca

Trenton Chamber of Commerce 97 Front St., Trenton, On K8V 4N6
(613)-392-7635 email: trentoncc@telos.ca

Northumberland County Tourism
860 William St., Cobourg, On K9A 3A9 (905) 372-3329 1-800-354-7050 ext. 237
email: tourism@eagle.ca   website: www.eagle.ca/tourism

Campbellford-Seymour Chamber of Commerce
Box 376, Campbellford, On K0L 1L0 1-800-268-4561 Phone/Fax:(705) 653-1551

Peterborough Kawartha Tourism and Convention Bureau
175 George St. N. Peterborough, On K9J 3G6 1-800-461-6424 (705)-742-2201

Lakefield and District Chamber of Commerce
Box 537 Lakefield, On K0L 2H0 (705) 652-6963

Victoria County Tourism
Box 9000 Lindsay, On K9V 5R8 Phone: (705) 324-9411 ext.233
email: countyvi@victourism.org   website: www.victourism.org

Bobcaygeon and Area Chamber of Commerce
Box 388, Bobcaygeon, On K0M 1A0 1-800-318-6173(ont.only) (705) 738-2202

Lindsay Chamber of Commerce
2 Kent St. W. Lindsay, On, K9V 2Y1 (705) 324-2393 Fax: (705) 324-2473
email: coc@lindsaytown.org

Scugog Chamber of Commerce 269 Queen St., Port Perry, On L9L 1B1
(905) 985-4971

Destination Barrie - Hotline: 1-800-668-9100

Orillia & District Chamber of Commerce
150 Front St. S. Orillia, On L3V 4S7   (705)326-4424

Midland Chamber of Commerce   (705) 526-7884

Penetanguishene/Tiny Chamber of Commerce
2 Main St. Penetanguishene, On L4M 1T1 (705) 549-2232 website:
www.huronet.com/chamb_commerce

North of Superior Travel Association
1119 Victoria Ave. E., Thunder Bay, On P7C 1B7 1-800-265-3951 (807) 626-9420
Fax: (807) 626-9421 Email: nosta@lu.ca

North Channel Marine Tourism Council
P.O. Box 70 Spanish, On, P0P 2A0 1-800-563-8719

Travel Notes
● ● ● ● ● ● ● ● ● ● ● ● ● ● ● ●

Index of Advertisers

Don't forget to order your copy of the **Rideau Waterway Boating and Road Guide**. Call us to order **1-800-324-6052** or send $9.95 plus $2.50 shipping & handling to Ontario Travel Guides, 382 Marguerite Ave. Ottawa, Ontario, Canada K1L 7W5